Use your brain to beat DEPRESSION

Use your brain to beat DEPRESSION

the complete guide
to understanding and tackling depressive illness

JOHN ILLMAN
SERIES EDITOR **RITA CARTER**

First published in Great Britain in 2004 by Cassell Illustrated,
a division of Octopus Publishing Group Limited
2–4 Heron Quays, London E14 4JP

A CIP catalogue record for this book is available from the British Library.

ISBN 1 84403 196 9

Design by D.W. Design
Printed at Toppan, China

Contents

Introduction

Most probably you have opened this book for a reason. It might be that you know someone who is depressed and you would like to help them, or perhaps you are wondering if you are depressed yourself. Maybe you *know* you are depressed and you want help.

In one sense you *cannot* simply help yourself. You cannot just pull yourself up out of depression because, whatever its underlying causes are – they could be anything from grief, miserable life circumstances or physiological illness, to a tragic childhood or even a genetic vulnerability – the immediate cause of depression is the way that your brain is working. Of course, the way your brain works *is* you – there is no separate "you" hovering to the side that can order your brain to work differently. Nor will any amount of cheerful exhortations to "relax", "think on the bright side" or "count your blessings" lift you out of the pit you find yourself in.

Despite all of this, you can beat depression. Most sufferers do not get effective treatment, but the vast majority of cases (75–85 per cent) who do get the right treatment respond well to it. This book will show you how you can access the resources you need – from within yourself, and in the form of therapy options which are available to you. It also highlights the many reasons treatment fails – all too often failures result from poor understanding or a lack of knowledge.

Part One: Depression explains the difference between normal sadness and clinical depression, and provides the tools to help you decide whether your present condition is one or the other. It also describes the biological mechanisms that create depression, the difference between anxiety and depression and it provides an overview of the types of treatment that can ease both.

Part Two: Cognitive behaviour therapy provides a starter-pack of CBT, which has been shown to be the most successful non-pharmaceutical treatment available. You can either use CBT alone or combine it with taking drugs. You may actually need to try several therapies, always taking the advice of medical professionals, to find what works best for you. Perseverance with treatment is a very important element on the road to recovery.

Part Three: Resources gives details of available antidepressant drugs – the different types, their effects and side effects – as well as providing further contacts and pointers to information which you may find useful. This book is not, on the whole, concerned with exploring the complicated social and psychological roots of mood disorder. Rather, we aim to give information and tools that will help sufferers find speedy relief from this cruel illness, and ensure that it does not recur.

Part One
Depression

passive and helpless. The act of identifying your condition as depression may be the first step towards regaining a sense of control over your life. (NB two situations where this is not possible are in the case of smiling depression and masked depression. See page 57.)

Signs and symptoms of depression

You may have severe depression if you feel depressed nearly all the time, on most days, lose interest or pleasure in routine activities and, in addition, you experience five or more of these symptoms over two weeks:

- Lose or gain a significant amount of weight
- Feel excessively sleepy or unable to sleep on virtually all days
- Markedly slow down and feel sluggish
- Lack energy and feel tired
- Experience inappropriate guilt or feel worthless
- Lose concentration and have difficulty making decisions
- Think about death or suicidal attempts

"It was a horrendous experience – an amalgam of fear and unhappiness and not knowing where to turn. I was tired all the time, but I couldn't sleep. I shut my eyes, but my mind was always alert. I developed a ravenous appetite for sweet things and piled on the weight because I never had the energy to go out. I was always crying and could never really focus on anything. And I felt so alone. There didn't seem any point to life."

Josie, 40, housewife

What about less severe forms of depression?

The term "severe depression" does not imply other forms of depression are trivial; they're not. A minor depression can have major consequences. Any depressive illness – from postnatal depression to "the winter blues" (Seasonal Affective Disorder) and from premenstrual syndrome to cancer-related depression – is potentially disabling and frightening. Various screening tests or questionnaires, such as the one provided opposite, can help to distinguish severe depression from a less severe form of depression. Don't take too long over each question, if you try it, as your first answer will almost invariably be the most accurate one. This questionnaire is *not* a diagnostic tool, but it may help establish where you are on the depressive spectrum. For a quick guide a "major depressive syndrome" may be indicated if five or more items are ticked in the column "more than half the days"; or if either item a), ("Little interest or pleasure in doing things") or b), ("Feeling down, depressed or hopeless") are positive, i.e., recorded on "More than half the days". Less severe illness may be indicated if items b), c) or d) are ticked as being applicable more than half the days or if either item a) or b) is "positive", i.e., applicable more than half the days.

You can also monitor the progress made once treatment has begun by repeating the excercise on a monthly basis during and after treatment.

Depression screening test

Tick in the appropriate column to the right, indicating how often you have experienced the following over the past two weeks:

	Not at all	Several days	More than half the days	Nearly every day
a. Little interest in doing things that would normally engage you	○	○	○	○
b. Feeling hopeless, nothing is worth trying – it won't work out	○	○	○	○
c. Difficulty falling or staying asleep, or sleeping excessively	○	○	○	○
d. Feeling tired, lethargic or without normal energy	○	○	○	○
e. Loss of appetite or desire to binge on food	○	○	○	○
f. Feeling that you are a failure or that you have let other people down	○	○	○	○
g. Reduced concentration, eg. unable to read a book or focus on a TV programme	○	○	○	○
h. Noticeably slowed movements, speech or thought – such that other people comment; or agitation – moving and fidgeting more than usual	○	○	○	○
i. Thinking of suicide, or that other people would be better off if you were dead	○	○	○	○

This test is not a substitute for medical advice and consultation. You should see your doctor if you believe you have depression.

I "pass", but am I depressed?

Ok, so you can confidentally say that you have all of these symptoms, but how can you be really sure that depression, and not just life, is getting you down? Try this simple experiment: think about why you feel the way you do. Is your job boring? Do you have money problems or a rocky relationship?....Now think about exactly what would be required to make it alright. Imagine your dream promotion, coming out of the blue. Imagine winning the lottery. Imagine your partner, miraculously, suddenly becoming the person you've always wanted to be with, right down to the smallest details. Elaborate the fantasy: "live" it in your head....

Now: be very honest with yourself. In that fantasy situation, would you really be happy again? Would your worries clear and your mood lift? Can you feel this happening even as you think about it? If that is the case, it suggests that your life may be the problem. The question *then* is: do you have the energy, ability and motivation to do anything about it? If you do, you're probably *not* depressed (depressed people tend to feel unable to take action to help themselves). You should take stock of your situation and take appropriate action. If you cannot see the way to do this, you might benefit from counselling or cognitive behaviour therapy (see Part Three: Resources).

But if you can honestly say that *nothing* could happen which would make you feel better, or that you are *so* sunk in despair and hopelessness that you could not possibly start doing anything to change your circumstances for the better, or that there's no point in even trying, then you're almost certainly depressed and need help. This may be difficult to accept. Denying the existence of depression, as in the case of Gary, (see opposite), is common.

Gary – in denial

I suppose I regarded depression like road accidents – as something that would never happen to me, only others. Looking back, I can see that I refused to accept that I was depressed at the start, and failed to recognize a number of tell-tale symptoms, such as waking up around 3am, and not being able to get back to sleep; alternately losing and gaining weight, extreme mood swings; and a feeling of isolation that led to a gulf developing between me and my family.

Extreme irritability at home and a lack of interest in the development of my three daughters did nothing to improve matters. I was quite happy to exist in my own world and my way of coping was to devote more time to my work. In effect, my wife became 100 per cent mother and 75 per cent father to my children. She began to feel that the situation was becoming intolerable and to question whether our marriage had effectively come to an end.

Eventually I went to see my GP who was most helpful and sympathetic. He arranged for me to see a psychiatrist the following week at a local clinic. My wife came with me and the consultation lasted over three hours – I had expected it to be 15 minutes....

I had become obsessive about finishing tasks no matter what the cost to my family or myself, had set myself almost unachievable goals, had become emotionally stunted and was obsessed about pleasing people – ironically at the expense of my family.

With the help of medication, counselling and therapy, my confidence began to return, my sleep pattern improved and I began to mend fences with my family before they became irretrievably damaged.

Different types of depression

Apart from differing degrees of severity there are also different types of depression. It is important to distinguish between the two main ones: 1) those that involve being down all the time, and 2) those in which periods of depression alternate with bursts of elation. The first type is known as unipolar depression and the second as bipolar, or manic-depressive illness.

The mood swings in bipolar disorder can be sudden, extreme and catastrophic. Someone in a manic or high phase may feel euphoric, full of grand ideas and behave impulsively, perhaps running up big debts or starting an affair. They may become angry or impatient about the failure of friends or colleagues to translate their grandiose ideas into immediate action. Depression is, however, the primary consistent symptom, and can bring deep, overwhelming despair, guilt, apathy and inability to completing even the simplest task.

The UK Manic Depression Fellowship (see page 168) says: "It often first occurs when work, study, family or emotional pressures are at their greatest. In women it can also be triggered by childbirth or during the menopause. The illness is episodic (occurs in phases). It is possible to remain well for long periods. Typically the key to coping with manic depression is an early diagnosis and acceptance of the condition."

Bipolar disorder is more clearly attributable to genetic factors than unipolar depression. For example, studies of identical twins (who possess identical genes) show that if one of them becomes depressed, there is at least a 50 per cent chance that the other will as well – but in the case of bipolar disorder, the likelihood of the two twins sharing the condition is an even more startling 75 per cent.[2] While this points to a strong genetic link, it shows that other factors play a significant role.

It seems that bipolar disorder, like other types of mental illness, does not occur because of a single genetic defect. Many different genes may interact with environmental or other factors to cause bipolar disorder. Research published by *The Lancet* medical journal in 2003 suggested that schizophrenia and bipolar disorder – traditionally regarded as unrelated to one another – may share an underlying genetic defect.[3] Studying the preserved brains of people with the two disorders, researchers found abnormalities in the genes that produce myelin, the protective coating around brain cells. In another study, also reported in 2003, researchers identified a specific gene that regulates sensitivity to brain chemicals such as dopamine, leading to the extremes of mood associated with bipolar disorder.

One of the problems with diagnosing bipolar disorder is that during the manic phase the person is unlikely to recognize that they have a problem – life seems just wonderful! In some instances it can take someone with bipolar disorder ten years to get a correct diagnosis. The screening questionnaire (see next page) was developed by Dr Ronald Pies, of the Harvard University Medical School, to help with diagnosis, but it is also now used by patients as a starting point in their discussion with their doctors. You may find it a useful excercise if you are considering seeking treatment for depression yourself.

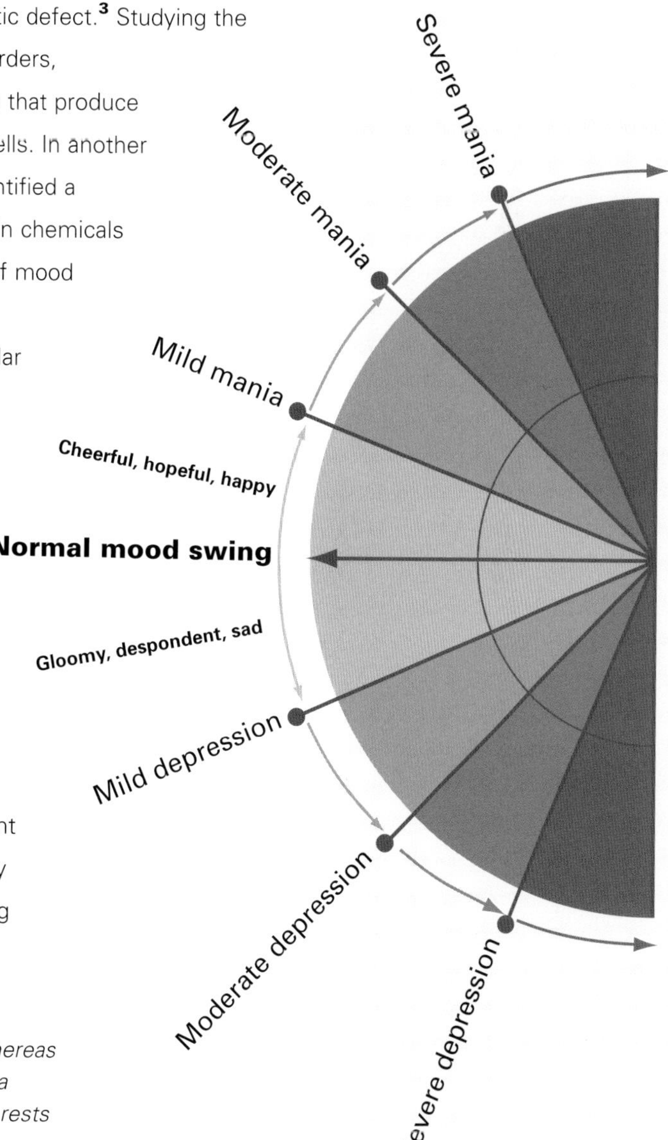

Bipolar disorder causes violent mood swings whereas severe (unipolar) depression is characterized by a persistently low mood. Most people's "needle" rests somewhere in between (see above right).

The bipolar spectrum diagnostic scale

Please read through all the statements once, then read the instructions that follow:

1. Some individuals notice that their mood and/or energy levels shift drastically from time to time. ☐

2. These individuals notice that, at times, their mood and/or energy level is very low, and at other times, very high. ☐

3. During their "low" phases, these individuals often feel a lack of energy; a need to stay in bed or get extra sleep; and little or no motivation to do things they need to do. ☐

4. They often put on weight during these periods. ☐

5. During their low phases these individuals often feel "blue", sad all the time, or depressed. ☐

6. Sometimes during these low phases, they feel hopeless or even suicidal. ☐

7. Their ability to function at work or socially is impaired. ☐

8. Typically, these low phases last for a few weeks, but sometimes they last only a few days. ☐

9. Individuals with this type of pattern may experience a period of "normal" mood in between mood swings, during which their mood and energy levels feel "right" and their ability to function is not disturbed. ☐

10. They may then notice a marked shift or "switch" in the way they feel. ☐

11. Their energy increases above what is normal for them, and they often get many things done they would not ordinarily be able to do. ☐

12. Sometimes, during these "high" periods, these individuals feel as if they have too much energy or feel "hyper". ☐

13. Some individuals, during these high periods, may feel irritable, "on edge", or aggressive. ☐

14. Some individuals, during these high periods, take on too many activities at once. ☐

15. During these high periods, some individuals may spend money in ways that cause them trouble. ☐

16. They may be more talkative, outgoing, or sexual during these periods. ☐

17. Sometimes, their behaviour during these high periods seems strange or annoying to others. ☐

18. Sometimes, these individuals get into difficulty with co-workers or the police, during these high periods. ☐

19. Sometimes they increase their alcohol or non-prescription drug use during these periods. ☐

Now that you have read this passage, please tick ***one*** of the following four boxes:

This story fits me very well, or almost perfectly. ☐

This story fits me fairly well. ☐

This story fits me to some degree, but not in most respects. ☐

This story doesn't really describe me at all. ☐

Now please go back and put a tick after each sentence (numbered 1–19 above) that definitely describes you. **Score one point** for each sentence ticked. Then, to this score add the following (depending upon which of the above four boxes you ticked):

Add **6** points if you ticked "fits me very well or almost perfectly"
Add **4** points if you ticked "fits me fairly well"
Add **2** points if you ticked "fits me to some degree, but not in most respects"
Add **0** points if you ticked "doesn't really describe me at all"

Your total score ____________

Likelihood of bipolar disorder is indicated by comparing your score with this guide:
1–6 Highly unlikely, **7–12** Low probability, **13–19** Moderate probability, **20–25** High probability

This scale is not a substitute for professional opinion and advice. Bipolar disorder shares symptoms with a number of other medical and neurological conditions.

Postnatal depression

Some types of depression are associated with particular events and the birth of a child can trigger a number of unwelcome feelings. Postnatal depression affects one mother in ten. Usually beginning in the first weeks after childbirth, it can last for weeks or a year or more. It should not be confused with "the baby blues", which affects at least half of all mothers, usually four or five days after childbirth. The baby blues usually subside within one or two days, with no lasting ill effect, but can develop into full-blown postnatal depression which can be very severe indeed. A new mother is quite likely to feel guilty for being miserable at a time associated with joy and celebration, and may not be willing to admit to her feelings. If the condition is severe, though, it is very important to seek treatment, because untreated postnatal depression can have a knock-on effect on the baby. There is concern that people whose mothers suffered untreated severe postnatal depression after their births are more likely to develop a depressive disorder themselves. In her book, *Feelings After Birth*, Heather Welford says: "Given that mothers are often the parent who is closer to the child, it would be astonishing if the mother–daughter relationship didn't have long lasting effects on the daughter's own experience of motherhood, and indeed postnatal depression."[4]

Seasonal affective disorder (SAD)

About 14 per cent of US adults report feeling less cheerful, energetic, productive and creative in winter. A further six per cent suffer from a disabling form of the winter blues known as seasonal affective disorder. Similar patterns exist in the UK and other European countries.

SAD is triggered by the changing ratios of light and dark, which set off a chain of hormonal reactions originating in a remarkable gland hanging in the middle of the brain. The pine cone-shaped pineal gland has intrigued scientists ever since it was acclaimed as "the seat of the soul" by the 17th century philosopher Descartes. As a result of its nerve connections with the retina, it is also known as "The Third Eye". The neurotransmitter serotonin, which plays a critical role in depression, is converted into melatonin in the pineal gland. Darkness is a signal to the pineal gland to make melatonin and light is a signal for it to stop. Thus melatonin provides the body with a biological time check. Until 1980 many scientists did not accept the hypothesis that light suppresses human melatonin. This held back the recognition of SAD – and delayed effective treatment.

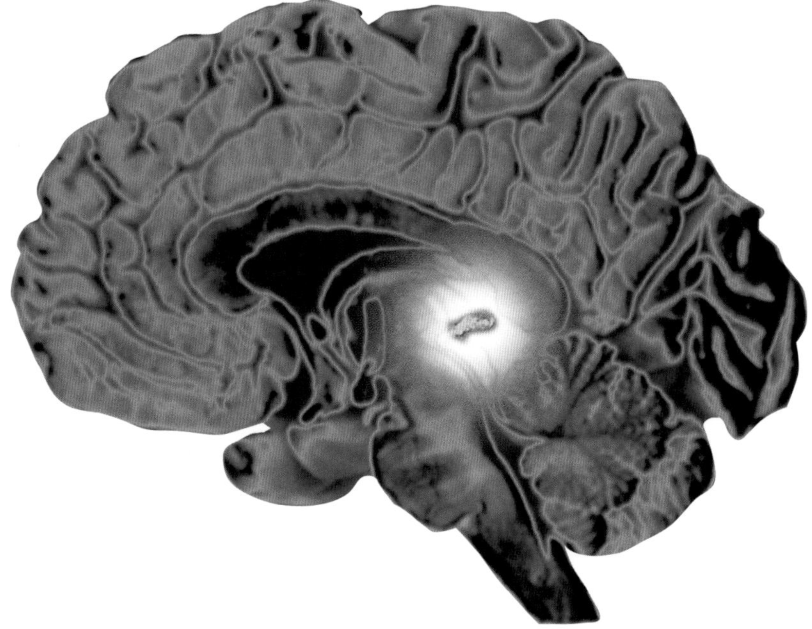

Shorter days in autumn set off a chain of hormonal reactions, starting in the tiny pineal gland (highlighted in this computer-generated image). It responds to light and dark, producing the so-called Dracula hormone, melatonin. Darkness is a signal for the pineal gland to make melatonin; light a signal for it to stop doing so.

Symptoms of SAD

- Disturbed sleep and early morning waking.
- Feeling of lethargy and fatigue and inability to carry out normal routine.
- Craving for carbohydrates and sweet food, usually resulting in weight gain.
- Irritability and desire to avoid social contact.
- Tension and inability to tolerate stress.
- Decreased interest in sex and physical contact.

"Whoever wishes to pursue the science of medicine in a direct manner must first investigate the seasons of the year and what occurs in them."

Hippocrates, father of modern medicine

The symptoms of full-blown SAD usually occur each winter, between September and April. The UK SAD Association says that a SAD diagnosis can be made after three or more consecutive winters of symptoms, which include those listed above.

Most sufferers are also more susceptible in winter to infections and other illness because they feel run down as a result of SAD.

Light therapy

Light therapy (using specially designed light boxes) works in up to 85 per cent of diagnosed cases. Ordinary light bulbs are not strong enough. Average domestic or office lighting emits an intensity of 200–500 lux, but the minimum dose necessary to treat SAD is 2500 lux. The intensity of a bright sunny day can be 100,000 lux. Light therapy can be combined with drug treatment.

CASE HISTORY:

Winter – The wild frontier

Winter no longer fills me with foreboding. All the evidence of its impending presence is still there in the world around me. But the feeling is different. There is a stirring inside me, a sense that this is what I've been waiting for, the winter, a wild frontier, alien and as familiar as the wilderness, provoking me to react, create, survive and triumph.

Don't get me wrong though. Winter still has the power to buffalo me. Every winter brings with it a few dark days when I feel a sort of stasis of the blood, a sludging of all biological processes, especially my thinking. I am in slow motion in relation to the rest of the world and compared to how I feel at all other times of the year. I have come to accept these days, but I still dislike them. I lose the capacity to process multiple things at the same time. I become linear. One idea has to be completed before there is room in my brain for the next one: one action at a time. Exercise is essential, coupled with light [therapy]. Yet motivation is hard to muster. I walk on my treadmill in front of the lightbox and the morning news.

By now, I have been through this cycle 20 times since my arrival in North America. I understand its biological basis, and more importantly that it will pass in time, provided I use light and exercise and limit the stresses that can be controlled. Above all, I accept my need to hibernate. I must let go of my driving demands. If I lower my expectations of myself, I have to acknowledge that my functioning is quite adequate, and for now, that has to be good enough.

The Christmas season brings with it its rounds of social activities. When I am not in my dark days, I am a very sociable person, but when the stasis of blood sets in, I want to sit at home, to brood and ruminate. Now it is time for some dinner engagement, and I am paralyzed before my clothes closet, fixated over what shirt to pick out, over the ordinary things that have to be done to get out of the house and on my way. "I have no energy, " I confide to my wife, "I don't think that I can possibly have any fun tonight."

"You always say that," she counters, "but you always do." She's right. People energize me. And so I am off again, carried forward by the remedies I both prescribe and use. And I do enjoy the parties, the friends, the fact that even though the sun has abandoned us again, there is life to be had in winter.

Norman E. Rosenthal, from *Winter Blues: Seasonal Affective Disorder, What it is and how to overcome it,* (pp 307–310), New York, Guilford Press, 1998

Bipolar disorder – two extremes

Interestingly, the late Spike Milligan spoke about a switch to describe his bipolar depression, in this interview with Professor Anthony Clare: [5]

MILLIGAN: It is like a light switch. I feel suddenly turned off. There is a tiredness, a feeling of complete lethargy. There may be something unexpectedly stressful – one of my daughters having a row with my wife, not talking to each other, something like that, which I find grossly unsettling. What I think should be occurring quite naturally, my wife and my daughter talking together, isn't happening and it upsets me and then I find I am getting depressed. Something like that might start it. It doesn't so much develop. It just goes bang like that and I find I am in the grip of it again and I just can't shrug it off. For instance, I had to fly to Australia to see my mother, who was ill. My brother suddenly decided, out of the blue, that I had been throwing away valuable family photographs. Finally he served me with a writ! The whole thing eventually smoothed over.
Then I gave my mother £400 to buy a washing machine. Unfortunately she became ill and had to go into hospital. He gave me back the cheque saying, "We don't want your money." Now I had been on pretty bad terms with him and I was pretty down, and this reinforced it. I don't know if that makes me depressed but it doesn't help.
CLARE: Would that sort of experience be enough to trigger a depression?
MILLIGAN: Well, it hurt damnably. But I am strong enough to take it now. But if I were to become a little depressed, that might be enough. It would be like a switch. I'd be gone. I'd be gone. A sort of hibernation.
CLARE: Some people might see this as a kind of escape — hiding away from trouble?
MILLIGAN: They would be wrong. It is no escape. It is a torture much worse than any problem you might face.

"And God said. 'Let there be light' and there was light, but the Electricity Board said he would have to wait until Thursday to be connected."

Spike Milligan

"A grief without a
pang, a void dark and
drear, A drowsy, stifled,
unimpassioned grief,
Which finds no natural
outlet or relief
In word, or sigh or
tear."
Samuel Taylor Coleridge, *Dejection*

Other famous sufferers

Richard II, Henry VI, George III, Queen Juana of Castile, Philip V of Spain, William Cowper, Ernest Hemingway, Graham Greene, Robert Schumann, John Ogden, Tracy Emin, President Abraham Lincoln.

Samuel Taylor Coleridge (far left): the British poet and contemporary of Wordsworth sought refuge in the house of a London physician as part of his fight against depression.

Queen Victoria (left): the imposing British monarch is reported to have gone into a deep depression after the death of prince Albert, which lasted 40 years.

Winston Churchill: Britain's wartime leader dubbed his bleak moods his "black dog". He was especially susceptible to depression during times of stress.

Edgar Allan Poe: there is much speculation that the father of the modern detective story suffered from bipolar depression.

Sylvia Plath (far left): the young American poet suffered from severe depression.

Vincent Van Gogh (left): the greatest of the Post-impressionist painters suffered from bipolar disorder.

Why do some people still deny depression exists?

A heart attack may be life-threatening, but it confers no shame on the individual. Depression, in contrast, still carries a stigma. A survey in the 1990s[6] revealed that:

- 71 per cent of the general population thought that mental illness was due to emotional weakness
- 65 per cent attributed it to bad parenting
- 45 per cent thought it was the victim's fault and could be willed away
- 43 per cent thought it was incurable
- 35 per cent thought it was a consequence of sinful behaviour

Only ten per cent of the sample thought depression had a biological basis and involved the brain, even though it had long been established that depression is as much a physical illness as heart disease or pneumonia.

Fortunately, more and more people are talking publicly about their own personal experience of depression and as a result public awareness of what being depressed really means is increasing. At the same time patients are being encouraged to play a more active role in their health care and to exercise choice over treatment. Although this is a huge step forward, it is not a cure-all – nor is it an easy option. Making decisions may be the last thing you feel like doing if you're in the trough of depression, but it becomes easier if you think through your options. This book spells out some possible options for you, which may help you to overcome the blindness that envelops so many of us when we become depressed.

2 Stress and distress

"Everybody has it, everybody talks about it, yet few people have taken the trouble to find out what stress really is.... Nowadays we hear a great deal at social gatherings about the stress of executive life, retirement, exercise, family problems....The word stress, like success, failure or happiness means different things to different people, so that defining it is extremely difficult."

Hans Selye, *Stress without Distress*, Lippincott and Crowell, 1974

Anxiety and depression

There is a lot of similarity between the symptoms of anxiety and depression and the two often occur together. In particular, depression often follows a period of anxiety. In a national survey in the US, 58 per cent of patients with a major depressive disorder were found to have a clinical anxiety disorder.[7] The two conditions are quite distinct, however. Put crudely, anxiety is a type of diffused fear which causes your brain to race with worry and the rest of your body to tense in preparation for action. It does not necessarily provoke action of any useful sort, and if anxiety is too intense it causes a sort of paralysis, or pointless fretting and jitteriness that leads to exhaustion.

Just as we all feel low at times without being clinically depressed or ill, we also experience anxiety without being clinically ill. Indeed, depression and anxiety can be healthy and even desirable. It would be surprising if we didn't feel depressed about the loss of a loved one or the loss of a job we enjoyed. Similarly, it would be surprising if we didn't feel anxious about an important exam. I feel anxious about writing this book, for example. This is, I believe, a perfectly normal response to a difficult task – an example of what Charles Kingsley, author of *The Water Babies*, called "divine discontent". To take another example and the consequences of an anxiety-free life, the anxiety-free speaker who steps fearlessly onto the rostrum will probably bore everybody but himself.

Though there is no clear cut-off point between healthy concern and potentially disabling anxiety or depression, generally speaking, some forms of mental stress are quite normal in the short term, though they cease to be so if they persist over weeks or months.

Depression or anxiety – a quick checklist

Use this to differentiate between feelings of anxiety and depression:

	Depression	Anxiety
Feeling	Low mood, sad, despondent, dejected	Tense, constantly feeling under pressure
Thoughts	Sluggish, characterized by poor concentration, indecisiveness and guilt	Racing, resulting in the mind going blank and a lack of perspective
Behaviour	Hiding away, clinging dependancy, no interest in leisure activities	On edge, restless, lacking control
Biological symptoms	Poor appetite or weight loss/ increased appetite or weight gain, sleep problems, low libido, feelings of agitation	Lightheadedness, clammy hands, shakiness, dry mouth, sleep problems, muscle tension

How does stress come into the reckoning?

Stress is usually thought of as something that happens to us – an assault from outside. But it is not that at all. Stress is generated by our *response* to things that happen, not by the events themselves. Hence something like moving house can be hugely worrying and unpleasant for someone who does not particularly welcome the change, while a person who has been longing for a move may find it exciting and joyous. Both people are experiencing stress, but in the first case it is debilitating and in the second it is energizing. Our response to potentially stressful events varies, too, according to our experience and genetic make-up. Some people crave constant change and novelty, and become stressed when there is too *little* going on around them. Others are easily unsettled by changing circumstances, and become anxious when something big happens even if it is supposedly "good".

How do you adjust to the inevitable chain of events which change the direction of your life? The "Social Readjustment Rating Scale" (see page 36) was designed to show the relationship between social readjustment, stress and susceptibility to illness. It lists the things which may trigger stress-related anxiety, depression or other illness, in the general population.[8] So-called "life events" such as getting a new job, going on holiday or getting married are each given a score. For example, divorce scores 73 points and taking out a large loan for a house, 31 points. The higher your total score, the higher your risk factor.

However the scale is a guide, not a "stand-alone" measure of stress. Divorce, for example, may not be especially stressful if the partners have been separated for a long time, and some people are more genetically susceptible to stress-related disease. Moreover, it can take years for stress to contribute to illness.

But tests did seem to confirm the validity of the calculations used in the scale. For example, of 2500 men aboard three Navy cruisers, the 30 per cent with the highest life-change scores developed almost 90 per cent more first attacks of depression during the first month of the trip than the 30 per cent with the lowest scores. During the rest of the mission, the high scoring 30 per cent consistently developed more illnesses than the lowest 30 per cent.

Nonetheless life events such as those on the rating scale are still only part of the story. "Minor" or "everyday" stressors – a late train or an irritating colleague – can also have profound repercussions. It is important here to recognize the imperfections within our brains which can contribute to depression and anxiety disorders. There has been, in effect, a head-on collision between evolution and what we know as progress. The body's stress response evolved to deal with short term "tooth and claw" emergencies in which our ancestors chased prey or ran from predators. This "flight or fight" response is not so good for the many people (most of us) who have to face the same situations, the same family, the same pressures, the same stresses, week in, week out. There is nowhere to run to; no effective way to fight off the threat and no dispersal of the adrenaline and feelings associated with preparation for fight. In short, our lifestyle may have changed, but our bodies remain much the same as they were thousands of years ago.

The compilers of the stress rating chart overleaf, Thomas H. Holmes and Richard R. Rahe of the University of Washington, calculated the following scores which you can use if you wish to judge your own stress levels:

- A score of 150 indicates a 50 per cent chance of developing an illness
- A score of 300 increases the chance to 80 per cent
- A score of less than 150 means you have no more than the average risk of illness.

"However confident we may be, when the time comes to make use of the health services, most of us feel we know nothing at all. At a time of stress and anxiety, we are only too willing to be led blindly, without any clear idea of what is happening to us, unable or too scared to find out."

Sarah Harvey and Ian Wylie, *Patient Power*, Simon and Schuster, 1999

Stress ratings

Events	Score or scale of impact	Your score
Death of spouse	100	
Divorce	73	
Marital separation	65	
Prison sentence	63	
Death of close family member	63	
Personal injury or illness	53	
Marriage	50	
Sacked from job	47	
Marital reconciliation	45	
Retirement	45	
Change in health of family member	44	
Pregnancy	40	
Sexual problems	39	
Gain of new family member	39	
Business readjustment	39	
Change in financial state	38	
Death of close friend	37	
Change to different line of work	36	
Change in number of arguments with spouse	35	
Taking out a large mortgage	31	
Foreclosure of mortgage or loan	30	
Change in responsibilities at work	29	

Events	Score or scale of impact	Your score
Son or daughter leaving home	29	
Trouble with In-laws	29	
Outstanding personal achievement	28	
Spouse begins or stops work	26	
Begin or end school	26	
Change in living conditions	25	
Revision of personal habits	24	
Trouble with boss	23	
Change in work hours or conditions	20	
Change in residence	20	
Change in schools	20	
Change in recreation	19	
Change in church activities	19	
Change in social activities	18	
Taking out a small mortgage or loan	17	
Change in sleeping habits	16	
Change in number of family get-togethers	15	
Change in eating habits	15	
Holiday	13	
Christmas	12	
Minor violations of the law	11	
	Total	

3 Depression: a physical illness

"Consultant psychiatrist Sally Pidd compares the brain to a battery, which to function properly, needs a conducting fluid of some kind to bridge the gap between two poles. 'What seems to be the case in depression is that there isn't enough of the transmitter substance between the interconnecting neurons of the brain'....But, and it's a big but, she adds: 'What people don't know is WHY this process should make people depressed in the first place. People will often say to me, "Can you do a test to see whether I'm properly togged up?" And the answer is no.'"

Trevor Barnes, *Dealing with Depression,* Vermillion, 1996

What is it that makes depression so painful?

Thoughts, memories and emotions – are *physical.* They are particular patterns of activity in particular brain cells (neurons), and, with the right sort of brain-scanning equipment, you can actually *see* them in the brain. In this way they are exactly the same as physical sensations. Indeed, one way to look at depression is to think of it as – literally – a type of pain.

"Ordinary" pain – the sort you get when you stub a toe – is produced by a particular area of the brain. It is called the anterior cingulate cortex, and it is a tiny bit of grey matter which nestles in the deep groove that divides the left and right hemispheres. A pain in the toe also involves other areas of the brain – bits that identify the type of pain, and the location of the injury – but it is the anterior cingulate cortex that makes us register it consciously. This has been shown by brain-scanning experiments. For example, there is a condition called "silent angina", which differs from "ordinary", painful angina in that patients do not have pain. Their heart arteries contract in the same way as other angina patients, but instead of feeling the chest pain that warns the others to rest, they feel nothing. Naturally, silent angina is more dangerous than ordinary angina because people who have it do not get a pain "alert" when their body is at risk. Brain

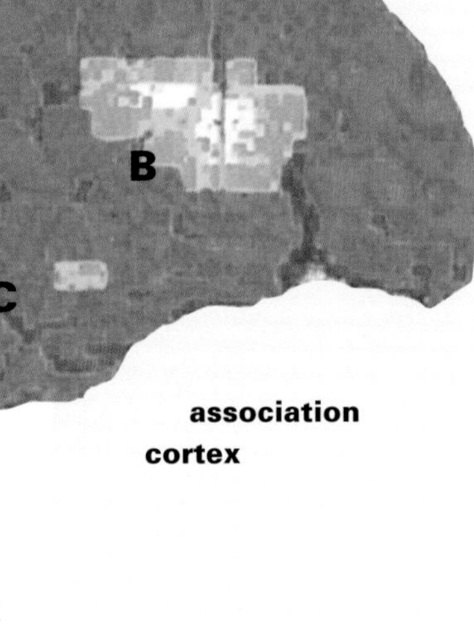

A – Pre-frontal cortex (thought elaboration)

B – Visual association cortex

C – Auditory association cortex

Emotions are physical – as is revealed by brain-scanning equipment. For example, the brain of a depressed person (right) shows less activity than that of someone who is healthy (above) in areas which affect emotion.

scans of "ordinary" and "silent" angina patients show that the only physical difference between them lies in their brains. In the first, the contraction of the arteries produces activity in the anterior cingulate cortex. In the others it does not. This (and other experiments) strongly suggests that pain – the conscious feeling of "ow!"– is generated here.

So how does this relate to "painful" emotions? Well, it seems that emotional pain is generated in just the same way as any other type. Researchers at the University of California in Los Angeles observed activity in the brains of a group of volunteers who had been duped into thinking that they had been intentionally left out of a ball-throwing game. The researchers compared the brain activity with that in another group who had been left out of the game – but in their case it had been made clear that the other players did not *want* to exclude them. In other words, the first group were feeling "hurt" while the others were not. The difference between them? In the first group the anterior cingulate cortex was active. In the second it was not. The "pain" of social humiliation was generated in precisely the same way as the pain from a physical injury.[9]

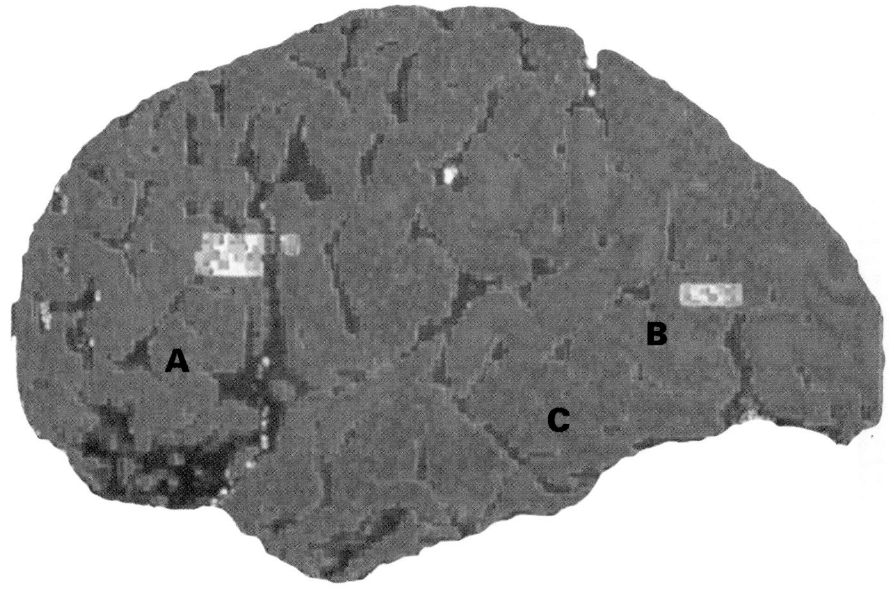

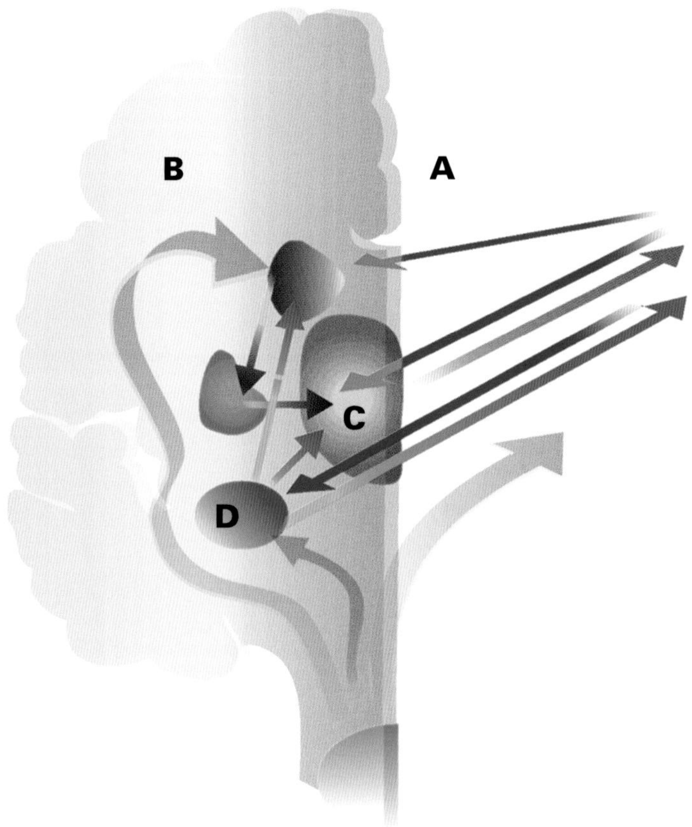

Some parts of the brain are over-active in depression and seem to form a vicious circle of negative feelings. These include:

A – The anterior cingulate cortex, which locks attention on to sad feelings. It is this part of the brain which seems to register pain – anything from ordinary pain when you stub your toe to "painful" feelings and emotions

B – The lateral prefrontal lobe holds sad memories in mind

C – The middle thalamus stimulates the amygdala

D – The amygdala creates negative emotions.

Going back to pain caused by physical injury – the angina example shows that sometimes the brain fails to produce pain when it would be useful for it to do so. Conversely, the brain can produce pain that has no source. The clearest example of this is phantom limb pain. People who have had a limb amputated often continue to feel sensations that seem to come from their missing part, sometimes for years after it has gone. Obviously, the pain is not "in" the amputated limb – it is being generated in the brain. The brain areas which were activated by sensations from the limb when it was attached, continue to be activated even though the signals have ceased to come in. It "remembers" the pain – and plays it back like a memory.

Depression is the emotional equivalent of this "learned" pain. The brain gets so familiar with the feeling of misery that it no longer responds to changing circumstances. It is locked into the negative feelings, like a person who is lost in past memories can no longer respond to the changing world. What is needed is to "unlearn" the memory – to nudge the brain back into responding differently, or thinking new thoughts. We will see that this is a *physical* process. New thoughts occur when new neural pathways are formed between brain cells. If thoughts are repeated these become permanent – like well-trodden paths through a wood. Old pathways slowly disappear if they are not used. "Unlearning" negative thinking therefore involves building new thought pathways and abandoning the old.

It takes time, and practice to establish a whole new pattern of thinking, which remains fragile for a long time. The majority of people who are treated for a first bout of depression relapse within two years of the initial attack. This is often because they abandon treatment as soon as it starts to work, and don't wait until the new thought patterns are physically well-established. We will be looking at drug treatment in more detail later, but it is worth noting here that the goal of the first six to eight weeks of antidepressant therapy is symptom relief. Guidelines suggest treatment should continue for at least four to six months to reduce the likelihood of relapse. Antidepressants act on brain chemicals, which is our next topic.

The chemical connection

Brain activity is brought about by the release of chemicals known as neurotransmitters. If you are ecstatically happy, your brain cells pump out neurotransmitters such as dopamine, noradrenaline, serotonin and oxytocin, and these produce a happy state by activating certain circuits in the brain.

Normally, neurotransmitter activity alters, moment-by-moment, according to the things that happen to us. If we see an attractive stranger looking at us, for example, certain neurons pump out dopamine and set up activity in what is commonly known as the brain's "reward circuit", which makes us feel excited and hopeful. These fluctuations keep our emotions flexible and ensure that our feelings are tuned to the needs of the moment.

In depression, this dynamic chemical system goes awry. Brain cells which produce feelings of pleasure fail to produce or respond to the neurotransmitters that usually turn them on, and thus become "dead" to outside stimulation – the attractive stranger passes by unnoticed.

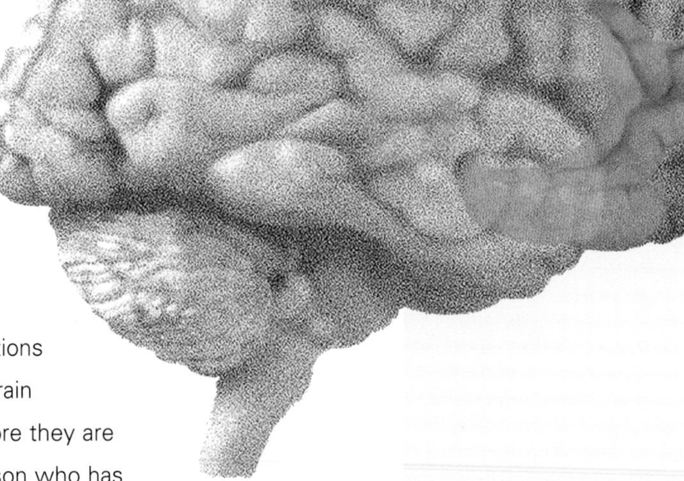

Some brains are more likely to suffer this sort of deadening than others, because of their physical structure. The brain is made up of interactive "modules" – areas which are responsible for different functions. The area that is largely responsible for feeling pleasurable emotions is situated in the front, left-hand side. Brain modules are like muscles in that the more they are used the bigger they become. So a person who has

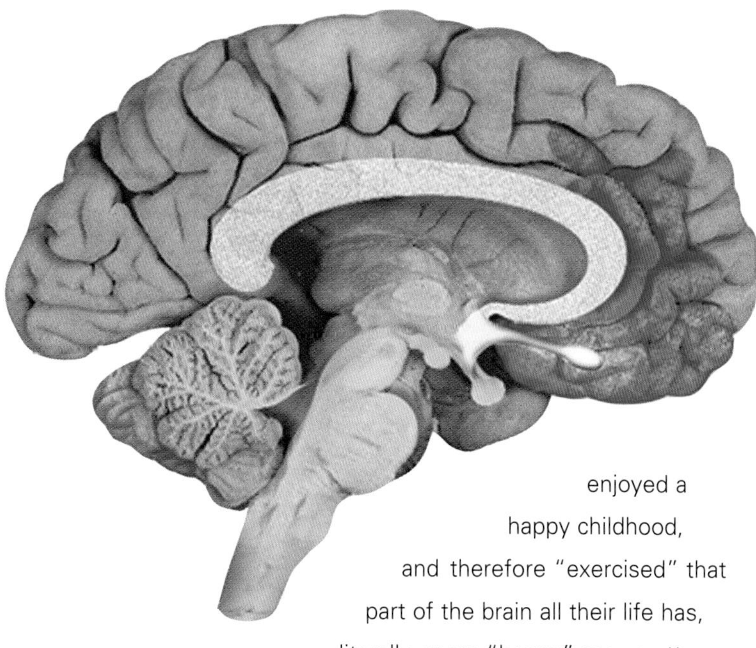

enjoyed a happy childhood, and therefore "exercised" that part of the brain all their life has, literally, more "happy" grey matter to activate than someone who has spent a large part of their lives feeling sad. Brain cells also die off if they are not used, so a person who suffers a period of intense sadness in childhood may lose some capacity to feel happy later on. This is one reason why depression should not be left to cure itself – people who do not get treatment are far more likely to suffer a relapse than those who nip it in the bud.

The parts of the brain that register and respond to outside events tend to be underactive in depressed people, while those dealing with internal feelings, particularly those that are painful or worrying, stay on full alert. These computer scans show the frontal cortex activity in a depressed person who is recalling taking part in a sporting activity. In a normal subject you would expect to see intense activity in the outer area (see far left) which is responsible for planning movement, and very little response in the "core" area (shown, top) – concerned with monitoring the body's internal state. In this subject, however, that pattern is reversed.

The limbic system

Pleasurable feelings are experienced when there is activity in part of the brain that lies just behind the forehead, but the *generation* of emotions starts in a deeper area of the brain, the limbic system. This sends and receives messages from the rest of the body and also controls body temperature, sleep–waking cycles and eating patterns. Emotional "messages" from the limbic system therefore affect all body functions – one reason why depression has such wide-ranging physical effects. The limbic system encircles the top of the brain stem and forms a border (the meaning of "limbic") linking the cortical and midbrain areas with lower centres controlling automatic, internal body functions.

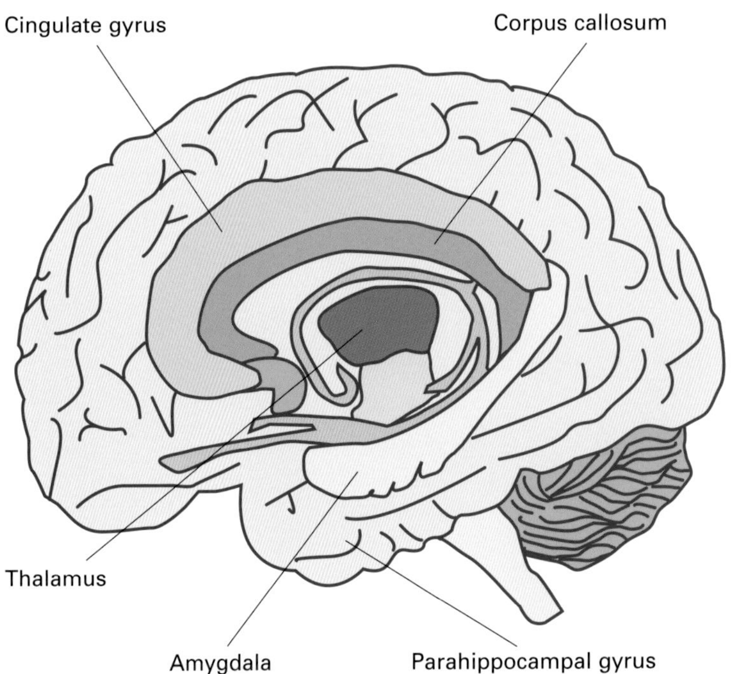

The **cingulate gyrus** *along with the parahippocampal gyrus and olfactory bulbs, comprise the limbic cortex, which modifies behaviour and emotions.*

The **amygdala** *registers and modifies emotional responses such as fear and anger.*

The **hypothalamus** *regulates food intake, blood flow, water–salt balance, the sleep–wake cycle and hormonal activity. It also receives messages from the amygdala, and helps prepare the body to cope with events that trigger fear and anger.*

The **corpus callosum** *bridges the gap between the two hemispheres of the brain, passing information back and forth to ensure that they work in unison.*

The **parahippocampal gyrus** *communicates with areas of the cerebral cortex – specifically those areas involved with sensory function.*

Location of the limbic system

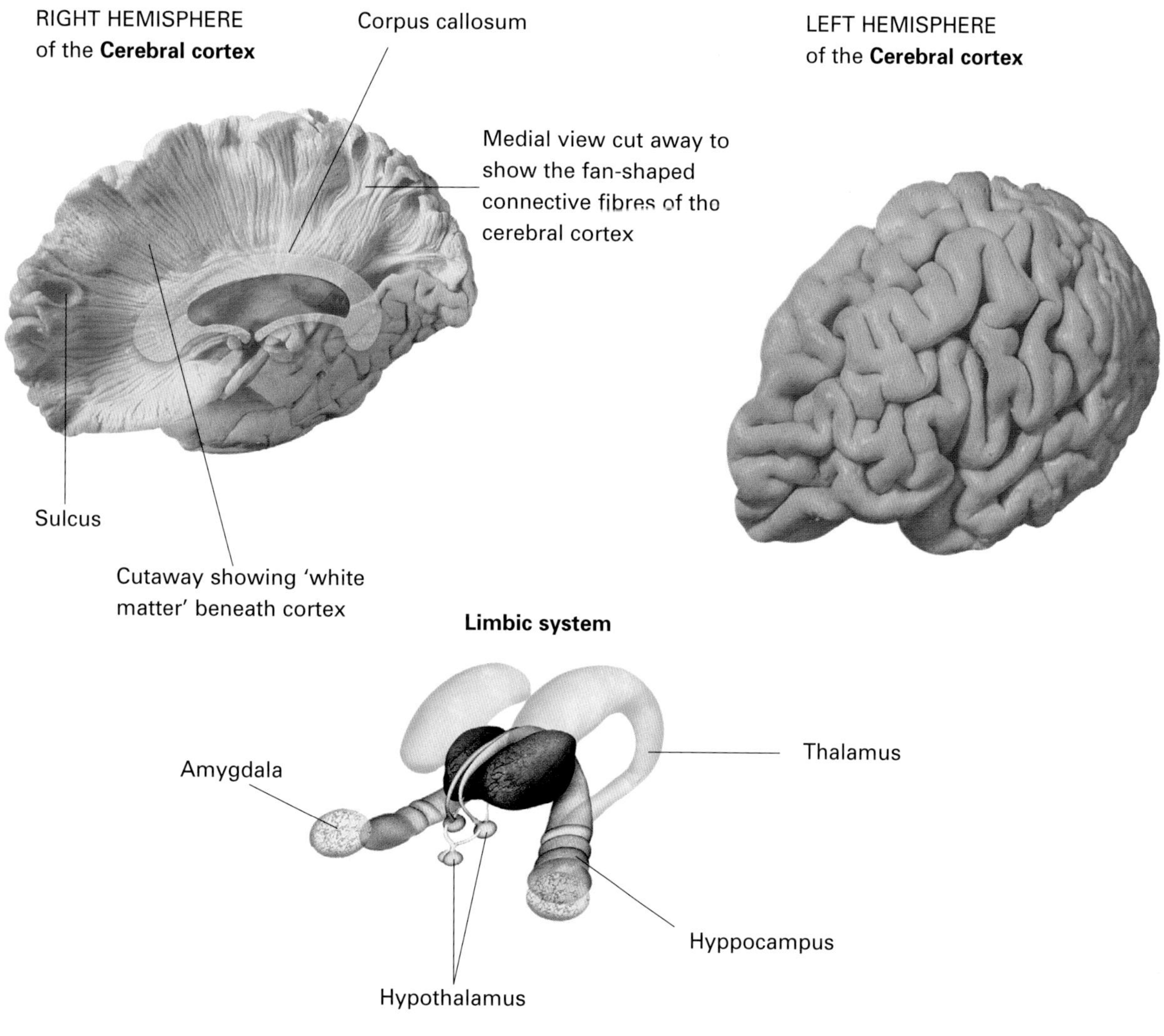

How does the brain's mood regulation break down?

Neurons – the basic unit of the nervous system – are communication specialists. They used to be thought of as simple on/off switches, but now they appear to be "little brains" in their own right. Each of the billions of neurons in your brain receives information from anything between one and a thousand others, in the form of electrical impulses. Instead of merely passing on this information, it sifts and prioritizes it, favouring input from "reliable" sources, ignoring that from others, and adjusting its output accordingly. Input and output of signals is controlled by branch-like dendrites (receivers) and elongated axons (transmitters).

When a neuron is stimulated, the wave of electrical disturbance (the nerve impulse) travels along the neuron at speeds of up to 100 metres a second. Most of these electrical impulses jump from one cell to the next across a tiny gap known as a synapse. The first part of the journey – to the end of the nerve fibre – is easy. The second part – across the synapse to the second cell – is where the going can get tough. The problem is in bridging the gap and this is where neurotransmitters (chemical messengers) come into play. When the impulse reaches the end of the first cell, it releases neurotransmitter chemicals into the synapse or gap. Some of these neurotransmitters lock onto matching receptors on neighbouring cells and some remain floating in the synapse and are broken down by enzymes. Others are scooped up and pumped back into the cell they emerged from.

Neurotransmitters carry signals to target cells. For example, dopamine sent out by a cell in the "reward circuit" signals the next one to fire up – and if the train of activity sparks far enough they will produce a conscious feeling of elation. But sometimes the signals do not get through – that is, they fail to lock on to neighbouring cells. Or they might lock on, but not get a response. Or there may not be enough dopamine to convince the second cell that it is worth responding. Or the second cell may be inundated with conflicting signals from other cells – signals which tell it to keep quiet – to which it gives priority.

So there are many ways that the brain can interpret information from the outside. To go back to the example of an attractive stranger: the brain

The millions of neurons in the nervous system carry electrical impulses that form a communication system which enables us to think, feel and act. The picture (left) shows two neuron cells separated by a gap – the synapse.

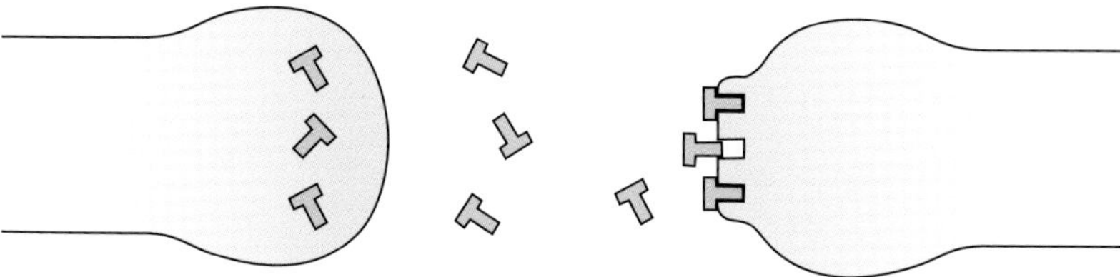

Neurotransmitters, such as noradrenaline and serotonin (see next page) bridge the gap between two neurons, resulting in a chain reaction which enables the nervous system to carry information throughout the brain and body.

is naturally inclined to feel a dash of excitement – but if the dopamine is not flowing, or some cells in the circuit fail to respond to it, or are inhibited by conflicting signals, the feeling is not aroused.

Depression is, of course, far more complicated than this type of momentary lapse of emotional response. But the essential mechanics – neurons failing to respond appropriately to events, or over-responding to negative ones – are similar. And because the system is mediated by chemicals, chemical intervention – drugs – can correct it when it goes wrong.

Neurotransmitters

The main neurotransmitters known to be involved in mood regulation are:

Serotonin (5-hydroxytryptamine or 5HT) is known as the "feel-good chemical", and it has a profound effect on mood and anxiety – high levels of it (or sensitivity to it) are associated with serenity and optimisim. It also helps to maintain appetite, sleep and sexual activity and our response to the changing seasons.

Noradrenaline (also known as norepinephrine) helps regulate energy and mood, both of which fall sharply in depression, and plays a key role in the body's response to acute stress. It is found in the nerves that connect the brain with the heart and blood vessels, and works in tandem with adrenaline. In response to an electrical brain impulse, noradrenaline is released from the nerve ending to stimulate the heart. The heart steps up its activity, providing more blood for the brain and muscles. As the body moves into emergency "fight or flight" mode, breathing becomes faster and deeper, providing more oxygen; increased perspiration cools the body. This "fight or flight" response to fear or anxiety is designed to withstand short-term emergencies, and was ideally suited for tooth-and-claw emergencies but is less well suited to the modern age.

Dopamine helps promote feelings of happiness and wellbeing and is found in the brain's "pleasure centres". Animals can be taught to press a lever and will continue to press it furiously if each press triggers a tiny electric shock to certain cells in these centres. Too little dopamine is known to cause tremor and the inability to start voluntary movement (Parkinson's disease and related disorders) and is implicated in feelings of meaninglessness, lethargy and misery (depression), social withdrawal and lack of attention and concentration.

"The countless millions who live with their depression are yet further proof, if this is necessary, that the human brain does not always run smoothly within itself."

Anthony Smith, *The Mind,* Hodder and Stoughton, 1984

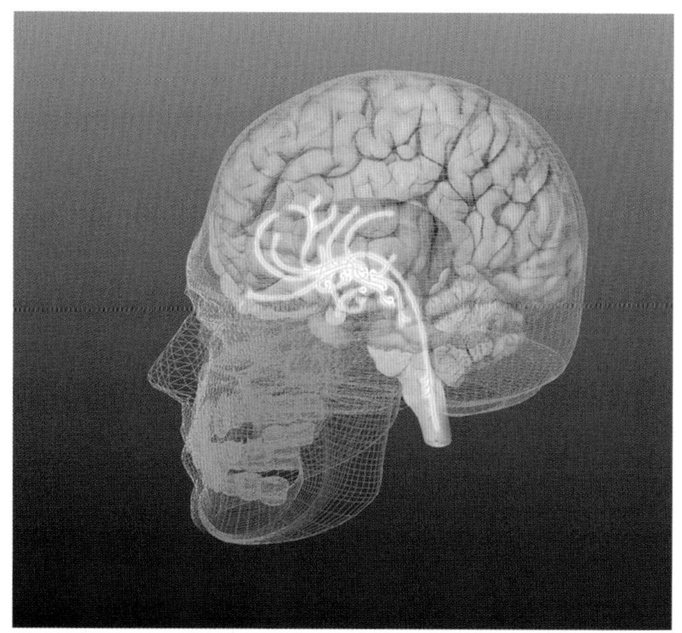

The information received from the senses or generated by thought is processed in many different parts of the brain. The dopamine pathways (left) and the serotonin pathways (below left) play a key role in the processing of this information. Serotonin helps to regulate mood and dopamine helps promote feelings of happiness.

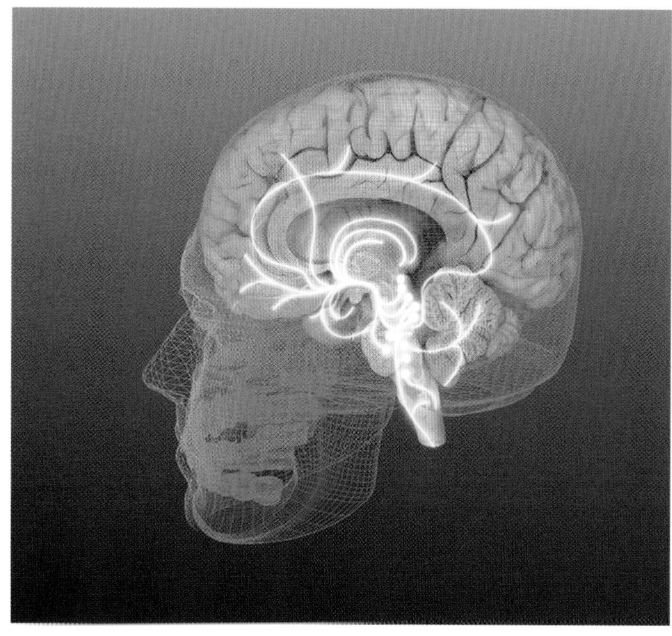

But what about 'nature and nurture'?

When asked to think of something sad women generate more activity in their emotional brains (top right) then men (bottom right). This suggests that women may have stronger emotional reactions to self-generated thoughts and memories.

Altered brain function is the *immediate* cause of depression in every case, but there are many underlying factors that may, in turn, cause these alterations. Risk factors include genetic susceptibility, psychological trauma, social circumstances and upbringing. In the short term it is probably not useful to focus on underlying causes because even if they are things that you can do something about, you are unlikely to be able to do it while you are depressed. Some things – genetic factors, for example, cannot be changed.

Genes

It seems people don't inherit depression directly from their parents, but that some genes can make them more susceptible. As noted earlier, studies of identical twins (with identical genes) show that if one becomes depressed, there's at least a 50 per cent chance that the other will also suffer. For non-identical twins, the risk is 25 per cent. As many as 20 per cent of a depressed person's relatives will develop some form of depressive illness. The risk for a child is about 50 per cent if both parents have depression.[10] But, even if you do have a genetic susceptibility you are unlikely to develop depression unless there is a trigger such as a psychol-ogical trauma or any of the other "risk factors" described in this section.

Hormonal changes

Women are four or five times more likely to be diagnosed with moderate depression than men (the figures even out for severe illness). This may be partly because women are more likely to take their problem to a doctor and thus be included in the statistics. Even allowing for this, though, it seems women are more vulnerable to mood disorders. One possible cause is female hormones.

Addressing the annual meeting of the Royal College of Psychiatrists in 2001, Professor Uriel Halbreich, of the Department of Psychiatry and Gynecology at State University, New York, said that fluctuating levels of oestrogen could lead to bouts of depression. These could happen at any time in a woman's life, from adolescence onwards.

He linked the days immediately after giving birth to withdrawing from a drug such as alcohol or heroin. Once the placenta was expelled, hormone levels – higher than at any other time in a woman's life – plummeted. "The sudden removal of the placenta is like the sudden withdrawal of a drug. It's a shock to the body and depression is a natural consequence," he said.

Proposing that oestrogen patches should be prescribed to help women beat "the baby blues and fight depression around the time of the menopause", he said that nine out of ten psychiatrists were unfamiliar with these hormonal mechanisms and gave women inappropriate treatment. Of course, not all women are affected in the same way.

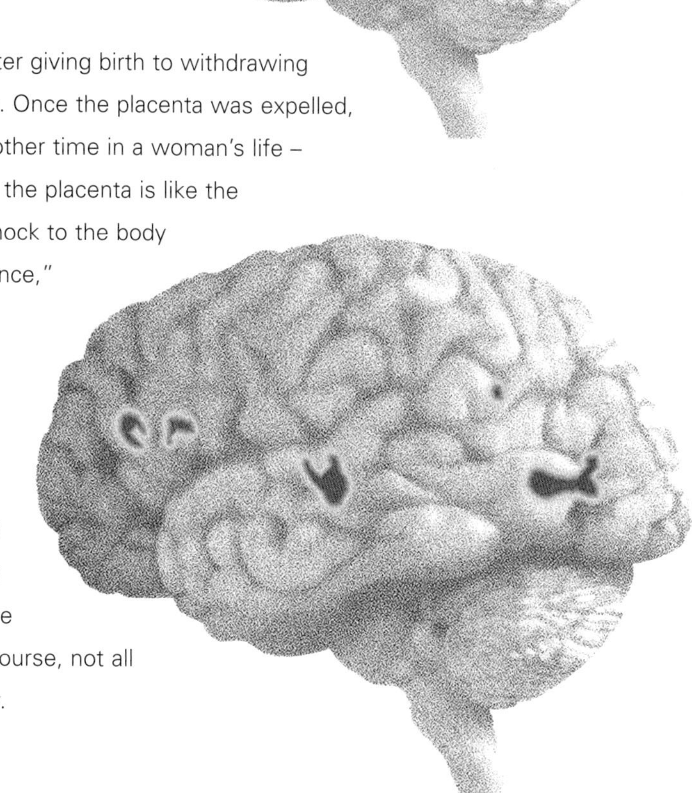

Childhood trauma

Neglect and physical and sexual abuse in childhood can also increase subsequent risk – as can losing a parent through death, disease or leaving home. Such events seem to prime the brain so that it is likely to overreact, in a negative way, to subsequent setbacks (see page 115). Psychiatrist Dr Tim Cantopher explains: "People don't tend to get ill the first time something bad happens. Children, in particular, will seem to cope with whatever you throw at them: they are wonderfully adaptive. For example, a 12-year-old girl who loses her father to cancer will not become obviously depressed. She may become clingy, fretful, or poorly behaved for a while, but in due course, if handled well, she will be pretty much back to her old self. There are apparently no problems, other than missing her dad. But then 20 years later she is made redundant from her prestigious and well-paid job, and rapidly develops a severe depressive illness."[11] In addition, children, like adults, are also susceptible to everyday stresses and strain – such as peer pressure, conflict with teachers, homework and exams and divorce and separation of patients. In *Stress and Depression in Children and Teenagers*, Vicky Maud quotes figures suggesting that depression affects at least two in 100 children under the age of 12, and five in every 100 teenagers. (See page 56 for more figures about students.) On the basis of her work as an agony aunt, Maud comments: "Bullying has to come close to the top of the list of causes, with thousands of children setting off to school each day, scared, unhappy and isolated. Many never tell their parents, or anyone else for that matter."

Depression and other illnesses

There is no real distinction between brain and body – what happens in one necessarily affects the other because they are all part of the same system. Depression is a "mind-body illness". Many illnesses can cause temporary mood disorders; conversely, mood disorders can cause organic illness. Some examples include:

- **VIruses** – especially glandular fever. Post-viral depression can last months, even years, but usually lifts dependant on rest and patience.
- **Thyroid problems** can cause hormonal imbalance. Located in the neck, the thyroid gland releases the hormone thyroxin. Too much speeds up metabolism, making the body "race", causing anxiety; too little causes sluggishness and depression. Doctors treat with thyroxine hormone tablets. Vitamin and mineral supplements may also help.
- **The menopause** is associated with depression. This may be due to social or personal problems rather than the menopause itself.
- **Cancer.** Having cancer is depressing enough, but cancer can also cause physical depression – as can cancer drugs and radiotherapy. Other forms of illness or surgery also increase risk of cancer.
- **Alcohol abuse** and depression are closely linked. Depression can drive us

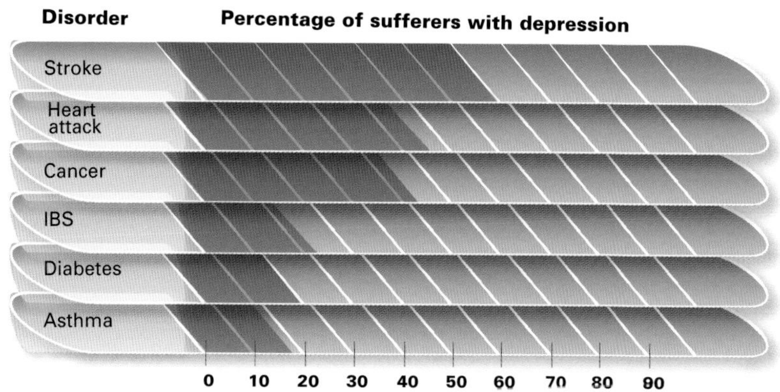

This chart shows the startling prevalance of depression as a secondary illness

to drink, but drinking can also cause depression. Alcohol may make people more sociable, lively and friendly, but behind its guise as a stimulant is, in pharmacological terms, a strong depressant – inhibiting the circuits that protect the brain from overload, it produces an increase in activity within the areas they usually modify or inhibit. Thus alcohol will bring a shy man out of his shell, or encourage a seven-stone weakling to biff a heavyweight bruiser. The effects are short-lived and prolonged drinking nearly always leads to deterioration in mood.

- **Heart disease.** The risk of heart disease may be increased by depression, research suggests, but this may be partly a result of the debilitating nature of untreated depression which often results in smoking, obesity, and failure to exercise and follow medical advice.
- **Stroke.** The same is true of stroke. In one 20-year study by the US Centers for Disease Control and Prevention (CDC), patients with symptoms of severe depression were found to have a 73 per cent increase in stroke risk.

Age, gender and depression

Depression can occur at any age to anyone, even in people in whom there is no obvious cause. Most sufferers have their first attack before the age of 30. Drs Aidan Macfarlane and Ann McPherson report that in one study, out of every 100 students:

- 61 freshers felt depressed sometimes
- 12 felt suicidal at some time
- 4 received treatment for depression
- 2 suffered from depression every day
- 1 in every 100 had attempted suicide [12]

Age and gender of depressed patients

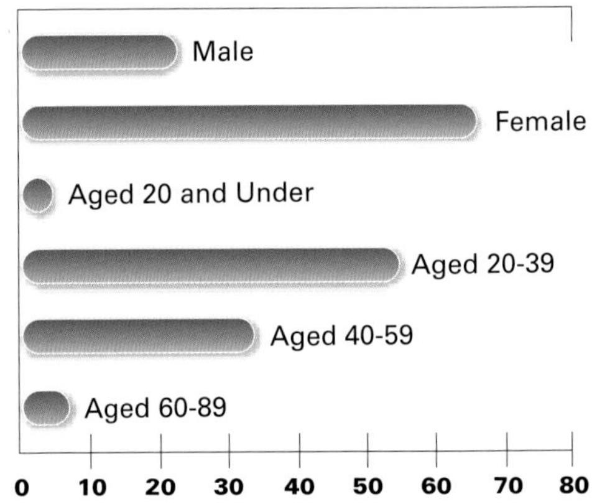

Masked depression/smiling depression

Strange as it may sound, it is true that depression can cause physical symptoms in the absence of any psychological sign that a person is feeling depressed. It seems as if such depression, expressed in physical symptoms proves that classic symptoms, such as feeling sad and worthless are only one part of the "depressive spectrum".

Common physical or psychosomatic symptoms associated with depression include:

- Backache
- Chest pain
- Dizziness
- General aches and pains
- Fatigue
- Indigestion
- Joint pains
- Loss of libido
- Palpitations
- Weight gain or loss

"Smiling depression" is a form of masked depression, whereby despite depression someone either consciously or unconsciously has "learned" to hide their depression behind a relatively light mood or expression. The British psychiatrist, Brice Pitt, says: "It is off-putting when someone who is seen by a doctor, for what seems like depression, smiles all the time. Perhaps they have that sort of face, or perhaps they have taken to heart that song 'Smile though your heart is broken' (although there may not be much gaiety in the eyes). A smile certainly does not rule out quite severe depression. The traditional British 'stiff upper lip' or 'putting on a brave face' under duress can lead the unwary doctor to underestimate someone's suffering."[13]

The depressed patient may not link their emotional state with their physical symptoms and may even vehemently deny any association between the two. The case history opposite highlights the classic, frosty response to the question, "Are you depressed?" – "Well, you'd be depressed if you were as physically ill as me". Alternatively, the patient may not want to admit to emotional symptoms because of the stigma of mental illness; or they may fear their complaint will be dismissed as being "all in the mind"; or they may not want to face up to their psychological symptoms – even to themselves. This problem is often exacerbated by the failure of GPs to ask the right questions to elicit depressive symptoms.

Small wonder so many cases of depression go undiagnosed. According to one recent report, as many as one in five new consultations in primary care (general practice) were for psychosomatic symptoms for which no specific cause could be found.[14] Psychosomatic complaints (not all related to depression) are among the commonest reasons for GPs' referrals to hospital.

The sadness that dares not speak its name

Most illnesses are honest. They arrive on your doorstep one day, with a small suitcase of symptoms, and they announce themselves. If you are lucky, they won't stay very long. You don't find chicken pox masquerading as rheumatoid arthritis. When you have influenza, you get a raised temperature, sore throat, runny nose – it's not hard to know when you've caught it, and to seek treatment. Depression is not nearly so honourable.

The first time, I developed a sore throat after going into a pub where the music was so loud you had to shout....I went to see my doctor who examined my throat, remarked that he couldn't see anything, but that I might have a mild case of pharyngitis. He sent me home with antibiotics.

Meanwhile I sank into a miasma of misery and guilt. It was all my fault, I decided, for smoking all those illicit cigarettes. I was having a year out before university. Most people get jobs or go travelling. I had had similar plans myself, but by now I had stopped getting up in the mornings. Where was the point? I was going to die.

The only glimmer of hope was a further appointment with my doctor. I told him the antibiotics weren't working. He took another look at my throat, shook his head in puzzlement and asked me a few questions about my background. A knowing look appeared in his eyes when he learned that I had left school now and was preparing to leave home. A time of great change and stress, he suggested artfully. Had I considered that I might be experiencing depression?

I took umbrage, not so much at the suggestion, but at his refusal to accept that my illness was real. I could feel it – every second of the day – a dragging, grating pain. Of course I was depressed! Who wouldn't be?

I wish I could report that some blinding insight led me to understanding that my mystery throat illness had been a case of depression masquerading as something else. It would have saved me a lot of mental pain. Unfortunately, I did not discover this, or that antidepressants (in particular, those which have a sedative effect) could help, until many years later.

emental-health.com

Hidden statistics

It is estimated that as many as three in four cases of depression are neither recognized nor treated – hence the concept of the "iceberg of depression[15] (see opposite). A minority of cases are attributable to "masked" or "smiling depression". Some groups of depressed patients are less likely than others to be correctly diagnosed:

- **The elderly:** In the US, a panel of experts convened by the National Institutes of Health (NIH) concluded that "more than 60 per cent of older Americans suffering from depression, a highly treatable disorder, are not receiving appropriate therapy". The panel attributed the problem to misdiagnosis by health-care professionals and patients' acceptance of "sad feelings" as a natural part of ageing.[16]

- **The young:** While the elderly are assumed to be susceptible to illness on account of their age, young people are thought to be immune on account of theirs. As noted earlier, four out of every 100 students are reported to have received treatment for depression.

- **Pregnant women:** Twenty per cent of women "scored high" on a standard survey of depression but, of these, only 13.8 per cent were receiving any counselling, drugs or any other treatment, according to a study at the University of Michigan.[17] The researchers believe this was because of a misconception that antidepressants are unsafe for pregnant women and foetuses. Another US study found that obstetricians were more likely to make a diagnosis of depression in a pregnant woman if they themselves had been clinically depressed.[18]

The iceberg of depression

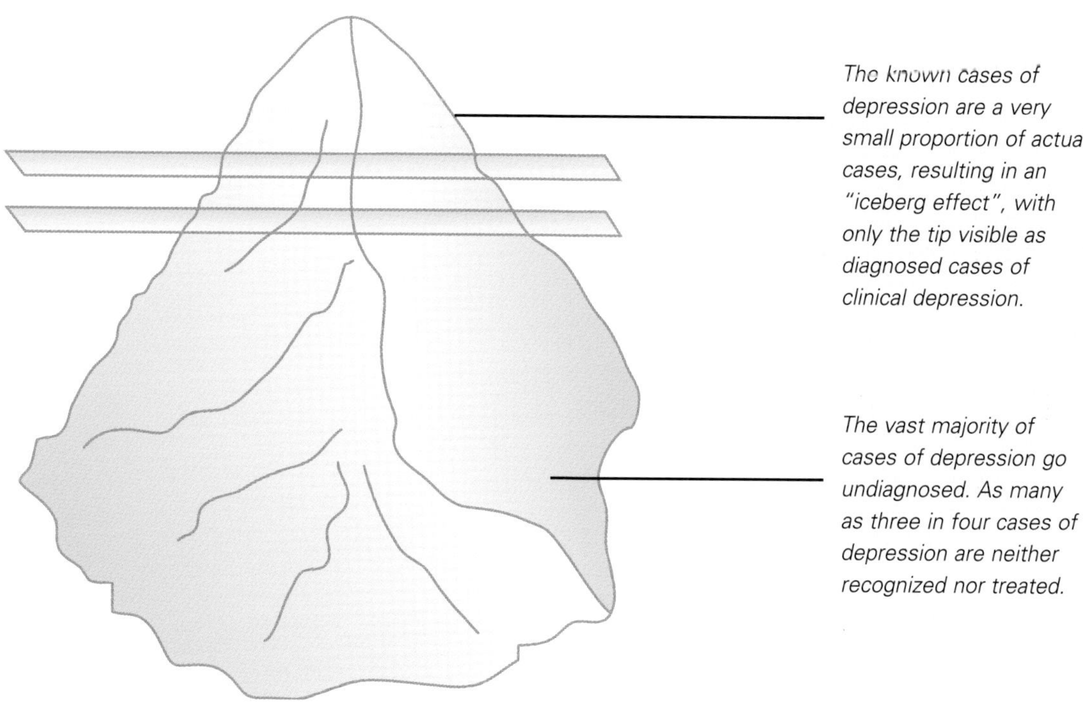

According to one estimate, about six per cent of men and 12 per cent of women suffer from depression each year. About one in 20 people at any one time suffer major depression.

4 You and your doctor

"The success of medical science has engendered a passivity in the minds of laypeople which has flattered the doctor's sense of power and self esteem. It has also caused people to assume less and less responsibility for what happens to their bodies and their minds and to ease doctors into the dangerous position where they privately come to believe they can control everything. The greatest benefit could come in the future if patients could take on more responsibility for their bodies and minds....Doctors then may come to acknowledge that...doctoring is something of a joint venture between patient and healer, in which the doctor serves as a guide."

Dr Glin Bennett, ***Patients and their Doctors,***
Secker and Warburg, 1979

Opening channels of communication

Doctors are specifically trained to diagnose what is wrong and, presumably, know about the iceberg effect, so why don't doctors diagnose more cases of depression?

Doctors are not robotic machines. They rely on patients to tell the truth – which they don't always do. Much is made of the unique nature of the doctor–patient relationship, and yet this special relationship is often characterized by lies and deceit. Most of us (if we're really honest) don't like to admit to emotional symptoms. It's very easy to talk about "the stigma of mental illness" as if it doesn't matter – but many sufferers will not talk about their depression to employers or colleagues for fear of being labelled as unstable, over-emotional or weak. Similarly, many clinically depressed patients stay away from the doctor or are too embarrassed or reluctant to talk about how they are really feeling. Ironically, doctors feature prominently in statistics for alcoholism, drug abuse and suicide, suffering far more from mental illness than the average patient. Suicide rates for UK doctors, for example, in the ten years up to 1998 were almost twice the national average.

It's worth repeating here that depression is as much a physical illness as heart disease or epilepsy. Try to be totally honest with your doctor. He or she is just another fallible human being who will (not unreasonably) probably take what you say at face value. The patient's code (opposite) provides a guide to make the consultation as easy as possible for both doctor and patient. Writing down all your symptoms beforehand, and anything else you need to remember, such as questions in the patient's code may make your appointment seem much less daunting.

The patient's code

- Prepare for the consultation. Write down all your symptoms and anything else worrying you – and take the list with you. It is very easy to forget important things during the consultation.
- Be honest. Don't leave things to chance in the hope they will suddenly disappear. Many people leave the doctor's without telling them about worrying symptoms.
- Be polite. Most doctors are not supermen and superwomen, but ordinary people trying to do a good job. Just like everyone else, they feel more inclined to make an effort for people who show appreciation. If you feel irritable or inclined to fly off the handle because you're worried or afraid, say so. It may help to break the ice.
- Respect your doctor. No one likes to be told how to do their job. An increasing number of patients are demanding treatments from doctors on the basis of information from the internet or the mass media. By all means discuss any information you have gathered. But ask your doctor which treatment he or she would want in your circumstances.
- Listen carefully. Most patients forget about half of what they have been told within a short time of leaving the doctor. Take written notes of the important points, or even better – if your doctor doesn't mind – tape record the consultation.
- Don't be afraid to ask questions. Doctors and patients are not good at communicating with one another, according to research. Doctors sometimes use technical terms patients don't understand and patients fail to say so – so doctors go on making the same mistakes. You may help your doctor improve his or her communication skills by asking questions if you don't understand them.
- Ask about groups that know about your condition. Ask your doctor or nurse for details of a relevant support group or voluntary health organisation which can help you get more information and help.
- Don't be afraid to ask for a second opinion from another doctor. You are within your rights to do so; there is no need to feel defensive about asking for one. But be polite about it.
- Don't be afraid to complain. Again, this is your right. Again, be polite. Most complaints against doctors are about rudeness and poor communication and are usually related to work pressure.

NB: You should complain if you feel your care has been sub-standard *regardless* of what you think the reasons may be.

So should patients be more assertive?

There's now much talk about the "expert patient", "the informed patient" and the "doctor–patient partnership", in which doctor and patient decide together what to do for the best. Partnership is perceived as the third way – steering a middle course between the paternalistic model in which the doctor decides what to do and the informed model in which the patient decides after considering the options available.

Of course these are just models: not necessarily representative of reality. As doctors and patients we play many different roles. It's easy to be a pro-active patient if you're fit and well – not so easy if you have newly diagnosed cancer or depression. Many a depressed patient has been grateful for an old-fashioned slug of paternalism.

But your doctor does not necessarily know what's best *for you*. Only you know what *your* depression is really like. A recurring theme in articles by doctors about their experience of disease is their sense of *surprise* about what it's really like to be a patient. The case history on the next page by a psychiatrist writing about his own experience of a major depressive illness is a classic example. In theory, he knew all about the side effects of antidepressant medication – as a psychiatrist he would have been regularly advising patients about them. But he was "surprised" by their severity and the memory loss after electroconvulsive therapy. He writes about how he hopes his experience will make him a better psychiatrist: make him more aware of patients' needs and fears.

This case underlines the need for anyone with depression to describe exactly their experiences as best they can, as everyone's case is individual.

The psychiatrist's story

Last year I was unfortunate enough to suffer a major depressive episode which required inpatient care and extensive physical treatment.... I hope that what I have observed, reflected upon and learnt will make me a better psychiatrist, more in touch with the needs and fears of my patients, and that my view of ward dynamics from the other side will give me more insight into why things happen as they do....

It seems that there is a price to pay in terms of side effects for the efficacy of any psychotropic medication, but I was surprised to find how bad these unwanted effects could get....It is easy for a depressed patient to become preoccupied with problems such as thirst, tremor and clumsiness, constipation or urinary retention, which may be bad enough to cloud the picture of an improving mental state. The staff should also bear in mind the effect the treatment as well as the illness may have on cognitive function, as this may be an added distress for a patient who cannot appreciate what is happening, or the fact that the impairment is temporary.

Despite having worked on a unit where ECT was often used I was totally unprepared for the magnitude of the memory loss I suffered, although I recognize that many patients experience only a transient short term effect, or none at all. I assume that the reason I did not become distressed about this until after the course was completed was that I began to try and think about things other than day-to-day life on the ward. I could not remember what my car or things in my house looked like, or what my job was, and when the time came for weekend leave, I was unable to find my way home.

Although my memory for faces remained intact, I could not remember the names of my friends, and I could not write Christmas cards for several weeks until the entries in my address book began to look familiar once again. My spelling was uncharacteristically poor, and the mistakes often involved substituting another word with the same sound but a different meaning. Regaining my memory was not a passive phenomenon, either, but involved a lot of persistence on my part and patient reality orientation by friends and relatives.

Anon, *Psychiatric Bulletin*

5 Drug therapy

"A drug can never be prescribed in isolation. It is always the result of an interaction between doctor and patient and therefore psychological factors are pertinent. A good doctor–patient relationship increases the likelihood of drug treatment being successful."

Alyson J. Bond and Malcolm H. Lader,
Understanding Drug Treatment in Mental Health Care, **Wiley, 1996**

How do antidepressants work?

Antidepressants seem to work by inhibiting or blocking the processes which lead to the destruction or removal of monoamines. These are the neurotransmitters responsible for activating brain cells which produce feelings of wellbeing. Hence the names of the two main families of antidepressants:

- **Monoamine oxidase inhibitors (MAOIs)**
- **Monoamine reuptake inhibitors. These include the tricyclic antidepressants (TCAs), the selective serotonin reuptake inhibitors (SSRIs), including Prozac, and selective noradrenalin reuptake inhibitors (SNRIs).**

The MAOIs block the enzyme responsible for destroying the monoamines, while the tricyclics and reuptake inhibitors decrease the absorption or "reuptake" of the monoamines into the cells from which they come. In other words they both achieve the same effect – keeping monoamines in the synapse – in different ways.

Given this, it is tempting to assume that depression is due simply to low levels of available monoamines, and that the cure is to push the levels up. There is something in this, but it is by no means the whole story. Neurotransmitter levels may be boosted within hours of a drug being taken, but something else has to happen before the raised neurotransmitter levels have an effect on someone's mood. As yet, no-one knows what it is.

The "something else" – perhaps some reordering of neuronal receptors or a change in cell structure – takes time. Because of this, antidepressant drugs do not start working immediately. People tend to feel better within one or two weeks but it may actually take longer to achieve a full antidepressant effect. Meanwhile, any side effects – which are common – may kick in quickly.

A cumulative effect

Feeling worse rather than better at the start of treatment leads many people, inevitably, to give up the drugs before they have a chance to do any good. Current evidence suggests that about half to two-thirds of patients with moderate or severe illness get relief from the first prescribed drug. The proportion goes up to 60–80 per cent if patients try a second or third type if the first does not work.

One of the key messages of this book is that successful treatment may mean trial and error. *The Maudsley 2003 Prescribing Guidelines*, produced in London by one of the world's leading psychiatric hospitals and research centres, lists some 20 different options for treating so-called "refractory depression" – depression that doesn't respond to treatment or which is hard to treat.[19] These options range from the tried and tested to other

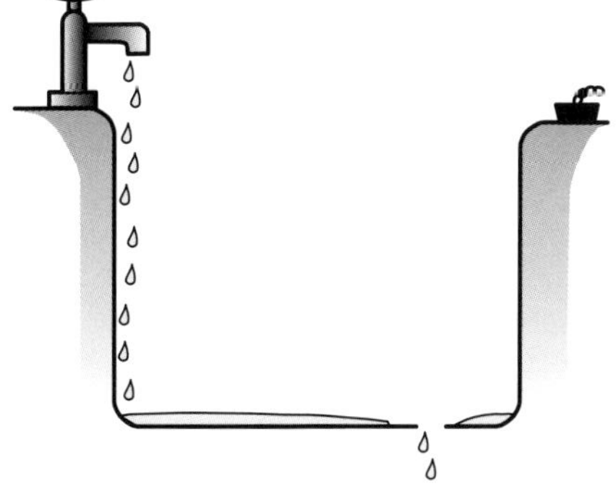

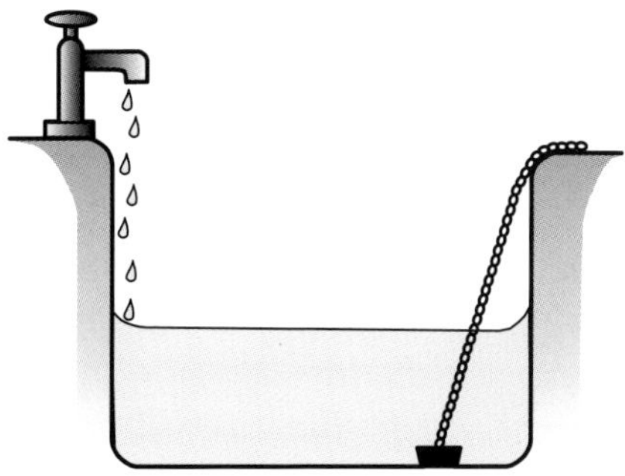

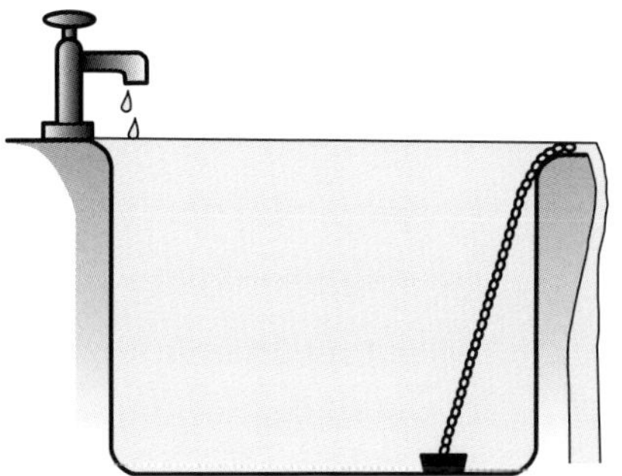

Wrong levels of neurotransmitters in the brain, associated with mood disorders, can be compared to a near empty sink in which the water level is restricted due to lack of a plug. In effect, this is what happens in depression. Antidepressant therapy provides a plug, ultimately restoring transmitter chemicals to the correct level. Surplus transmitter chemicals in the brain are directed to a "biological overflow" pipe to prevent excess levels building up.

regimes which may be worth trying but which are not well supported by research.

Such "last-resorts" may involve single drug treatments which may not be used initially because they produce side effects in large numbers of patients or require special monitoring. For example, blood pressure monitoring is essential for patients taking the SNRI Venlaxafine (see page 163), one of the newer antidepressants. Combination therapy, with two drugs working on different parts of the brain, may be tried if a patient does not respond to a single antidepressant.

By way of a dramatic example of combination therapy, US psychiatrist Andrew Morrison describes the case of "Alice [who] had experienced side effects on one of the new generation drugs and liked it better than any of the others she had tried before. 'No thanks,' she said. 'I'm doing OK. I've been on the others. This works just as well, if not better, and has fewer side effects. I don't want to try anything different.'"

But her doctor persuaded her to combine her new generation antidepressant with one she had been on before. This produced a "robust response" – within three months she was playing golf weekly, attending church and having friends over for dinner.[20]

Why do people say antidepressants don't work?

There are several reasons why antidepressants do not, in general, deliver the 75–90 per cent success rate that studies suggest they could. (See next page for some common reasons.) In addition, it is important to recognize that different types of drugs suit different people. At least a quarter of patients will not respond to the first one they take. At present there is no way of knowing what will work for whom, so prescribing is a hit-and-miss affair. Patients may be reluctant to try a second, or third drug, if the first fails. Many people initially suffer unpleasant side effects, stopping their drugs before they have time to work and deciding against trying another type. Moreover, family doctors (though not psychiatrists) are reported to prescribe antidepressants at too low a dose, and for not long enough, for them to become effective.

A survey[21] of 200 GPs in the UK found that only five per cent were following prescribing guidelines drawn up by the British Association for Psychopharmacology (BAP), with nearly a third following no guidelines at all. Moreover, of the GPs questioned, only 13 per cent said that they would treat for more than six months, and just 36 per cent for up to six months. The BAP guidelines recommend that treatment should continue for at least six months from the point that the patient's mood is the same as it was before they became depressed. Other guidelines specify treatment should continue for four to six months. Without treatment from this point, it is estimated, between one quarter and one third of patients will relapse into depression.) In another survey, only six per cent of UK health authorities were found to have completed the protocols and surveys governing mental health prescribing.[22]

Common reasons for failing drugs

Not knowing how long it takes for an antidepressant to "kick in". You wouldn't expect to walk normally within days of breaking an ankle. The healing process takes time. It's the same with depression – there's no quick-fix. Antidepressants take three to four weeks, on average, to start working – some drugs take six to eight weeks. However, many people stop treatment after a few days, assuming it's not working, especially if the prescribed drugs cause troublesome side effects, as mentioned on page 73.

"I'm cured". Some patients suddenly stop treatment, believing themselves to be "cured" because their symptoms have disappeared. This means that the treatment is working; not that you should stop taking it. Similarly, many people stop taking antibiotics prematurely, only to see their symptoms return. Stopping antidepressants abruptly can cause a relapse or serious withdrawal symptoms. *The British National Formulary,* "the prescribing doctor's bible", recommends continuing treatment after remission for at least four to six months – 12 months in the case of elderly patients. People with recurrent depression need "maintenance therapy" (usually in the form of reduced doses) for at least five years, possibly indefinitely (see page 84).

Genes and environment. It would be a lot simpler if we were all exactly alike, but we're all individual and respond differently to different treatments. Genetic and environmental influences account for wide variations in our individual responses to drugs.

Inadequate dosing. There may be a delicate balance between a dose

"Antidepressant drugs are effective in the treatment of major depression of moderate and severe degree, including major depression associated with physical illness and that following childbirth; they are also effective for dysthymia (lower grade chronic depression). Antidepressant drugs are not generally effective in milder forms of depression, but a trial may be considered in cases refractory to (resistant to) psychological treatments."

The British National Formulary, 46, September 2003

that's high enough to be effective, but not so high as to cause unwanted side effects.

Inappropriate prescribing. Antidepressants don't often help cases of mild depression. (See quotation, left.) More than 80 per cent of doctors in a 2004 UK survey by Norwich Union Healthcare admitted over-prescribing antidepressants. GPs said that "the appropriate psychological therapies... for mild to moderate mental health problems were not available."

Lowering the dose without proper advice. Some patients do this in the hope of avoiding side effects, if they're curious to see what will happen, if they're not sure if they want to take the drug at all, or if they want to exert more personal "control" over treatment. Guidelines for prescribing are carefully worked out on the basis of trials involving thousands of patients, but consult your doctor if you believe your dose is too high.

Upping the dose. More isn't necessarily better, but with most antidepressants there is a critical dose below which they do not work, and it differs from person to person. Don't increase a dose without consulting your doctor – it may cause dangerous, even life-threatening side effects. But if the treatment isn't working and your doctor suggests a higher dose, it may be worth giving it a go.

Taking medication at the wrong time or forgetting to take it at all. The treatment might not work if you don't get the right amount of the drug at the right time. Two patients out of five are reported not to take drugs as instructed, often as they don't understand or remember medical instructions, Taking notes or even recording the consultation helps.

"The doctor is trying to fob me off with pills": If you don't agree with your doctor's prescription of pills, discuss this with him/her. If you are still unsure you should get a second opinion or change your doctor, if possible.

Can the side effects be worse than the illness?

It's not so long ago that about half of all prescribed antidepressants were thrown away or abandoned because people just couldn't tolerate them.[23] The odds of experiencing side effects that make treatment intolerable is now less than one in eleven, according to one estimate. Although there is no way of knowing in advance if you will suffer any side effects from a particular drug, the newer antidepressants (reuptake inhibitors – SSRIs/ SNRIs) are generally less troublesome than the old ones (the tricyclics and the monoamine oxidase inhibitors). See the drug directory (page 154) for a detailed analysis of the different types of widely available drugs, their advantages and general disadvantages.

About one in four users of antidepressants are reported to experience side effects, the most common of which are shown opposite. Waiting several weeks for an antidepressant to "kick in" while unpleasant side effects occur straightaway is distressing. They may even seem worse than the illness, but the important point to remember is that they should not last more than a week or two. If the side effects persist, or are particularly unpleasant, go back to your doctor. Most side effects are dose related and doses can be adjusted to suit your body and lifestyle. The range of drugs now available means that a suitable, tolerable drug can almost always be found.

Side effects

Most side effects are temporary, but some persist, and it is a matter of weighing up the pros and cons – deciding whether or not the benefits outweigh the adverse effects. Common side effects include:

- Nausea, vomiting, dyspepsia (indigestion), abdominal pain, diarrhoea, constipation, dry mouth, nervousness, anxiety, headache, insomnia, tremor, dizziness, asthenia (lack of strength), drowsiness, visual disturbances and sexual dysfunction. (Insomnia and sexual disfunction may persist.) Antidepressants may also affect driving and other tasks involving machinery.

Always read the label

The patient information leaflets that accompany antidepressants list so many potential side effects that many patients are put off starting medication at all. It is important to read these leaflets in proper context. Drug companies are legally obliged to list all the significant side effects associated with their products – irrespective of how rare they may be.

Writing about the "new generation" antidepressants – which include the SSRI's – in *The Antidepressant Sourcebook*, the US psychiatrist Andrew L. Morrison puts the odds of having to stop treatment because of side effects at less than one in eleven. He adds: "Now compare that one out of eleven with the nine or ten out of eleven who will improve with antidepressants and psychotherapy. This is a fabulous trade off."[24]

Do SSRIs cause sexual problems?

Early reports suggested that sexual problems were rare with Selective Serotonin Reuptake Inhibitors (SSRI's), but this does not now appear to be the case. While they continue to produce fewer side effects on the whole than the older drugs, this is one area of health which people generally complain about during taking the drugs and throughout the treatment. Research suggests that most antidepressants may cause a loss of libido. In one survey up to 50 per cent of patients taking SSRIs reported a decline in libido after starting medication.[25]

SSRI-related sexual problems such as loss of libido are underreported because patients are embarrassed to talk about them, and yet there may be a simple solution. Decreasing the dosage may improve sex-drive while maintaining an effective antidepressant effect. In one study, nearly three-quarters of patients whose SSRI dosage was halved reported improved sexual function without loss of an antidepressant effect.

This underlines again the importance of honest, open medical consultations. You may find it difficult to talk about sexual problems with your doctor, but you may need to take the initiative. Drs Robert L. Phillips and James R. Slaughter, of the University of Missouri Columbia School of Medicine, warn: "Discovery of sexual problems is further limited by the frequent failure of physicians to ask about such problems," They say: "The latter point is critical. In one study it was found that patients taking selective serotonin reuptake inhibitors were four times more likely to reveal sexual dysfunction if asked directly by their physician."[26]

A final key point: loss of libido is a common symptom of untreated depression. Treating depression may actually *increase* libido.

Aren't antidepressants addictive?

Many people believe antidepressants are addictive, which, technically speaking, they're not. Antidepressants are often confused with benzodiazepine tranquillizers – which definitely are addictive. In a MORI poll in 1992 for the UK Royal College of Psychiatrists, 46 per cent of respondents classified antidepressants as addictive, a figure close to the 56 per cent who rightly put tranquillizers in the same class.

There remains, though, some controversy over whether or not antidepressants are addictive. The problem lies in the strict medical definition of "addiction" and the way the word is used colloquially. The medical definition states that an "addictive" drug causes "tolerance", i.e. the brain needs more and more of it to maintain the desired effect. This is what happens, for example, with drugs like heroin and cocaine.

Antidepressants *do not* cause this kind of tolerance or craving. You don't need higher and higher doses to maintain the same effect unless, as can happen, the depression "breaks through" the medicine. This occurs when the dose is no longer high enough to work – but this is more likely due to fluctuation in the underlying condition than a tailing off of the drug's efficacy.

One marker of an addictive substance is the occurrence of physical withdrawal symptoms when it is stopped. Some people suffer a recurrence of depression after stopping antidepressants, but this may be the original illness reasserting itself. However, many antidepressants cause clear withdrawl symptoms that are quite different from depression or anxiety. It is important to distinguish physical from psychological dependence or addiction. Anyone who is psychologically "hooked" may feel unable to function normally without a particular drug and will derive no comfort from reassurance that their drug is "non-addictive" or that what they're experiencing is "all in the mind".

I'm 23. I started taking Seroxat five years ago...I wanted to come off it for quite a few years, but when I stopped taking it I was so ill that I had to start taking it again. Doctors kept telling me it was impossible to be addicted to them, so I didn't know what was wrong, and I carried on taking them....It's taken me nine months to wean myself off it completely and that's been nine months of feeling ill for the majority of the time.

BBC website, March 2004

As one sufferer explained: "It's easy to regard antidepressants as 'a safety net'. If something then goes wrong, you may attribute it to the fact that you're not on the antidepressant anymore." Worry and anxiety may then give rise to physical symptoms such as sweating, nausea, chest pains, trembling and shaking – to name but a few.

The term "discontinuation syndrome" describes symptoms that occur when a patient stops taking a non-addictive prescribed drug. It affects at least a third of patients coming off antidepressants, according to one estimate, usually within five days of the last dose. The symptoms may be completely new or similiar to some of those of the illness. Mild symptoms usually subside within a few days. See your doctor if symptoms are severe.

There have also been reports that shortly after starting antidepressant therapy, some patients become uncharacteristically violent or suicidal. Those making the allegations are no more able to conclusively prove the link than the manufacturers are able to deny it. Given the millions of people taking SSRIs, it is statistically likely that some will be unstable, so the drugs may not necessarily be to blame. But there does seem to be a link between increased suicidal risk and the start of antidepressant therapy.

In Britain, the Committee on the Safety of Medicines (CSM) carried out no fewer than three reviews into suicidal behaviour and its possible link with SSRIs between 1991 and 2000. In a statement, the UK Medicines and Healthcare Products Agency said: "The CSM has concluded that the current evidence is insufficient to confirm a causal association between SSRIs and suicidal behaviour and advised that the issue should be kept under review. Product information for prescribers and patients contains warnings that suicidal behaviour may increase in the early stages of treatment with any antidepressant."

A more recent investigation by the US Food and Drug Administration into suicides by young people who had recently started on SSRIs concluded some antidepressants cause agitation, anxiety and hostility in a few patients. The extent of the risk, it added, has yet to be established.

It's always darkest before the dawn

If you have just read the last section, you may well be wondering why it is that people commit suicide after starting antidepressant therapy. Isn't this the very time when you'd expect to see a recovery and lightening of mood?

People in the trough of a severe depression may quite simply lack the energy to kill themselves. But when their energy starts to return, they may find the emotional means to kill themselves. Taking up this theme in *Dealing with Depression*, written with the Samaritans, Trevor Barnes says: "It is one thing to sit it out through an emotional winter, to be marooned in the dark loneliness of a chronic depressive illness. God knows, that is bad enough. But then to have the curtain drawn back for just long enough to see a tantalising chink of spring sunshine which may be blotted out as capriciously as it first appeared is too much for many to take. So it is at the very moment when bleak winter is giving way to an uncertain spring that some individuals take their lives. Far from being encouraged by the lure of health they are simply reminded of the depth of their sickness and find it impossible to have to go through all that again."[27]

Thus, paradoxically, just as they start to feel better, as their antidepressants start working, a small minority of patients may be at increased risk of suicide. Reports about suicide risks generate fear and alarm among patients, but the risk of not taking antidepressant therapy may be even greater. The case history (page 83) of Professor Lewis Wolpert highlights both potential benefits and risks. He has been taking a controversial antidepressant, Seroxat, also known as Paroxetine (see also page 163).

There are approximately 4500 suicides in England and Wales each year – about one in 100 deaths.

Up to 90 per cent of people who commit suicide have a mental health problem.

Alcoholics are most at risk of suicide (15 per cent of total figure) and people with diagnosed depression (15 per cent of total).

Mental Health Foundation report, 1997

Checklist for suicidal tendencies

It's sometimes hard to tell if someone is suicidal or depressed, as people in crisis react in different ways. However, there may be clear warning signs. This is The Samaritans' checklist:

Recent history: Has your friend:

- Had a recent loss (a loved one, pet, job)?
- Had a major disappointment (failed exams, missed job promotions)?
- Had a change in circumstances (retirement, redundancy, children leaving home)?
- Had a physical/mental illness?
- Made a recent suicide attempt? Also, is there a history of suicide in the family?
- Begun tidying up their affairs (making a will, taking out insurance)?

Visual clues: Is your friend:

- Withdrawn or low-spirited?
- Finding it difficult to relate to others?
- Taking less care of themselves?
- Different in some way, for example unusually cheerful or tearful, or trying hard not to cry?
- More irritable? Finding it hard to concentrate? Less energetic? Eating less (or more) than usual?

Things to listen for: Does your friend talk about:

- Feeling suicidal (it's a myth that people who talk about it don't do it)?
- Seeing no hope in the future or no point in life?
- Feeling worthless, a failure?
- Feeling very isolated and alone?
- Sleeping badly, especially waking early?
- Losing their appetite, or eating more than usual?

"Talking about feelings can make all the difference between choosing to live or die. Ask the person how they are feeling and listen to the answer. Encourage your friend to seek help and talk to someone they trust. Remember it's difficult to support someone who is suicidal on your own – encourage your friend to seek emotional support and talk to someone they trust – maybe friends, family, medical services, Samaritans. Contact us yourself."

The Samaritans, 2003

The professor's story

Seven years ago, aged 64, I had my first attack of depression – the worst experience of my life. It was set off by anxiety about a minor heart problem. The result was terrifying. I was suicidal and hospitalized. My psychiatrist put me on Seroxat and, very slowly, I began to recover. It took several weeks in hospital and another month at home before I could consider returning to work. It was a great strain on my family as, like all depressives, I was totally negative and self-involved. I was happily married and a professor at the university. With the help of cognitive therapy, I recovered and came off the drug. Four years later I had another depressive episode, possibly triggered by fear of retirement from my job. I went back on Seroxat, and managed to continue working, with difficulty. I remained on the drug, but on a very low dose, for about a year, and then, in 2001, the depression returned.

This time I didn't feel depressed but nauseous and ill. My psychiatrist was sure I was depressed and expressing it in physical symptoms. After four months on Seroxat, I recovered and now take a low dose daily. At present, I'm doing very well, and am often asked if the Seroxat is working. I cannot tell, but I don't intend to try to find out by stopping taking it.

There are indeed side effects, and these are listed in the leaflet that comes with the drug, but perhaps not enough emphasis is put on reports of increased agitation and possible suicidal thoughts when the drug is first taken. These antidepressants are not addictive, but one needs to come off them slowly. Patients should be warned about this, and also that there is an increased danger of suicide at the early stages of recovery, when there is the energy to carry out any suicidal intentions. I will continue to take Seroxat, probably until I die. I cannot face another attack of depression.

Lewis Wolpert

How long will my treatment last?

Many people have no idea how long they will have to take antidepressants for and there is little knowledge that they are often prescribed as part of maintenance therapy after they have started working. As a general rule, once a patient is symptom-free, treatment should continue for four to six months, or about a year in elderly patients. Recurrent depression is best treated with maintenance treatment for at least five years, possibly indefinitely.[28] (See Part Three: Resources for further information about treatment.)

The *Maudsley 2003 Prescribing Guidelines*, produced by the South London and Maudsley NHS Trust, report that:

- If antidepressant therapy is stopped immediately on recovery, half of patients will experience a return of their depressive symptoms.
- The risk of a recurrence is anyway high.
- In the case of recurrent depression, long-term treatment has been found to reduce the risk of symptoms returning by about two thirds. This benefit was found to last for more than three years in one "meta-analysis" of continuing long-term treatment.
- Antidepressants do not lose their effectiveness over time.
- They are not known to cause new long-term side effects.
- Stopping medication must not be done suddenly because this can result in unpleasant effects.[29]

"All experience convinces me and my family that severe depression is best treated by anti-depressant drugs. Devoted nursing by my wife saved me. My business was saved by other members of the family. I can now make films, write and lecture again. All the symptoms have disappeared. I no longer think I am going to die any minute. I can work a long hard day and my anti-depressant medication has been cut to a low maintenance dose."

Personal case history, from *the Guardian*, London, March 8, 1994

If your depression does return once you have stopped taking the drugs you should wait a week or so to see if it is simply a transient phase. But do not wait too long. The signs and symptoms of first and recurrent attacks are often the same, so learn to recognize the danger signals and restart treatment quickly. A rule of thumb which is worth repeating is that you should always consult with your doctor before starting and stopping treatment with antidepressants.

Specialists believe that treating depressive symptoms until they have disappeared may do far more than beat the blues. According to one idea, depression may be an integral part of other psychiatric disorders and have a long-lasting effect on the brain. Treating it may therefore reduce any other potential threats.

Many people don't like the idea of long term antidepressant maintenance therapy, but maintenance therapy is routinely used to treat heart disease, high blood pressure, asthma, diabetes and HIV/AIDS, among other things. So why not depression?

6 Electroconvulsive therapy

"Throughout the discussion concerning electroconvulsive therapy, we see the remarkable...tendency for practitioners, patients and members of the public alike to adopt a posture of absolute faith or incorrigible antagonism, and to adhere to such a position with a fervour comparable to that accompanying a religious conviction."

Anthony Clare, *Psychiatry in Dissent: Controversial Issues in Thought and Practice,* Tavistock Publications, 1976

ECT has had a really bad press but is this justified?

Electroconvulsive therapy (ECT), one of the most controversial treatments in medicine, involves passing a carefully controlled electric current through the brain via electrodes applied to the scalp. Introduced in the 1930s, it used to be given without anaesthetic and caused gross convulsions, but patients now receive an anaesthetic and muscle relaxant. The current is also much more carefully applied. ECT only seems to work if the current triggers a seizure. Originally it was applied in such a way as to bring about a major seizure, but nowadays the aim is to produce mini-seizures in particular areas of the brain. This section underlines conflicting views by different professional bodies over the potential risks of ECT.

The dread of ECT was highlighted by the distinguished psychologist Stuart Sutherland (see page 91 for his case history). No-one really knows how it works, but the UK Royal College of Psychiatrists said: "Over eight out of ten depressed patients who receive ECT respond well to it. In fact, ECT is the most effective treatment for severe depression. People who have responded to ECT report that it makes them feel 'like themselves again' or 'as if life was worth living again'. Severely depressed patients will become more optimistic and less suicidal. Most patients recover their ability to work and lead a productive life after their depression has been treated with a course of ECT."

Some patients may be confused afterwards, but the Royal College says that this generally clears up after an hour or so. It advises patients: "Your memory of recent events may be upset, and dates, names of friends, public addresses and telephone numbers may be temporarily forgotten. In most cases this memory loss goes away within a few days or weeks, although sometimes patients continue to experience memory problems for several months."

No clinical treatment is entirely risk-free. In each case it is a matter of evaluating the potential benefit against the potential risk. Unfortunately again, there is no way of predicting which patients are likely to suffer significant memory loss as a result of ECT. The question of the patient's autonomy to make their own health and treatment choices has become a central part of the ECT debate. ECT can be an invaluable stop-gap for the time between when a patient starts taking an antidepressant and when it starts working. But there is nonetheless considerable disquiet about ECT.

In 2003, the UK National Institute for Clinical Excellence (NICE) recommended that ECT should be used only after other treatment options had failed and/or when the patient's life was considered to be at risk. Its recommendations covered patients with:

- Severe depressive illness
- Catatonia (a form of schizophrenia)
- A prolonged or severe manic episode.

One team from the Institute of Psychiatry in London dismissed the statement by the Royal College of Psychiatrists that over 80 per cent of patients are satisfied with ECT and that memory loss is not important. It concluded that at least a third of patients undergoing ECT report "significant memory loss" after treatment; and that there was "controversy as to whether treatment was beneficial and whether patients are satisfied with it". The Institute team added: "Patients' views have never been systematically reviewed."

NICE's decision was welcomed, though, by the National Association of Mental Health (MIND) which carried out a survey of ECT among patients. More than 400 patients were included in the survey. Almost three-quarters (73 per cent) of the respondents reported that they had not been given any information about possible side effects, and more than half (52.5 per cent) said that they were not aware that they could refuse treatment.

MIND ECT survey results

- 40.4% of respondents reported permanent loss of past memories and 36% permanent difficulty in concentrating.
- 84% of respondents said that they had experienced unwanted side effects as a result of having ECT.
- A third (32.5%) of recent recipients felt hopeful before having ECT but 29% felt terrified and 22% felt that they were being punished.
- In the long term, 43% of more recent recipients felt that it was unhelpful, damaging, or severely damaging.
- Almost three quarters (73%) were not, as far as they remember, given any information about possible side effects.
- Over half (52.5%) were not aware that they could refuse to give consent to treatment.
- Only 8% had the opportunity to consult an independent advocate before making a decision about ECT.
- Depression was by far the most common diagnosis amongst respondents (53%).
- 66.5% would not agree to have ECT again.

"Some people find ECT helpful, and they should not be prevented from choosing this treatment provided they have been given full information."
MIND

Margaret Pedler, Head of Policy Development at MIND, and author of the report said: "This report confirms many of our worst fears concerning ECT. It is clear that people are still not being given enough information about...side effects, and this means that those who are giving their consent to ECT are not doing so out of an informed choice."

MIND believes that, for those people for whom ECT is being considered, there should be a legal requirement for an independent advocate, and an information leaflet that has been nationally agreed with all relevant parties, including service users. This leaflet would need to include information on side effects.

ECT

On my ward, several patients were transformed by ECT while I was there. Half-way through my stay someone was brought in with severe paranoid delusions. He believed that money was the root of all evil and refused to use it; in addition he thought there was a great conspiracy against him. One night when I was telephoning, he hung around, interrupting my every word. He heard me saying: "I'll see you tomorrow' and was convinced I was in a plot against him, saying "I know you're in it with all the others. You're going to attack me tomorrow – don't deny it, you're plotting on the telephone. I heard you plainly. Who's that you're phoning?"

Three weeks later, after six ECT treatments he was outwardly composed and cheerful and could talk interestingly and rationally. Four weeks after admission, he became a day patient, spending most of the day at the hospital, but returning home each evening: within three months he was back at work.

Although administration of ECT is now painless, it is still feared, perhaps in part because the tradition of how unpleasant it used to be has been handed down from one generation to another. On my ward there was usually an unnatural silence when preparations were being made for it, and although one rarely knew beforehand who was to be the recipient, he or she could always be identified afterwards by the small strip of sticking plaster covering the vein on the back of the hand where the anaesthetic had been inserted. Patients wearing such sticking plaster were treated with great solicitude by the others.

Stuart Sutherland, former professor of psychology at the University of Sussex

Part Two
Cognitive behaviour therapy

"The thinking man's psychotherapy"

1 New ways of looking at thoughts and feelings

"This new approach to emotional disorders changes man's perspective on himself and his problems. Rather than viewing himself as the helpless creature of his own biochemical reactions, or of blind impulses, or automatic reflexes, he can regard himself as prone to learning erroneous, self defeating notions and capable of unlearning or correcting them as well. By pinpointing the fallacies in his thinking and correcting them, he can create a more self-fulfilling life for himself."

Aaron T. Beck, *Cognitive therapy and the Emotional Disorders*, Penguin, 1989

Psychotherapy and early CBT

Cognitive behaviour therapy (CBT) is a kind of psychotherapy combining cognitive therapy and behaviour therapy. It gives a much simpler explanation of emotional problems than psychoanalysis, changing the way we think and what we do, which impacts directly on how we feel.

Psychotherapy sets out to change or modify:

- Feelings
- Perceptions
- Attitudes
- Behaviour
- Cognitions (thoughts)

In psychoanalysis, the first form of psychotherapy, Sigmund Freud (1856–1939) attempted to explain the patient/client's condition by analyzing their past and unconscious. Critics say classical psychoanalysis focuses too much on the problem (and the *past*) and not enough on the solution (and the *future*). "Neo-Freudians" have made psychoanalysis more "*present-and-future*" orientated.

Behaviour therapy, developed by John B. Watson (1878–1958) and B. Frederick Skinner (1904–1990), focuses on what we *do,* rather than what we *think.* Concepts like the "unconscious mind" cut no ice with the early behaviourists who maintained that thoughts and emotions were irrelevant to the study of human behaviour. John B. Watson is known as the father of behaviourism, which switched the dominant force in psychology from thinking to learning – from the study of consciousness to observable behaviour.

Watson's hope was to be able to predict and control behaviour and both him and Skinner were influenced by the famous series of reflex experiments with dogs by the Russian physiologist Ivan Petrovich Pavlov (1849–1936). Our mouths water or salivate when we smell food – it's a simple reflex response. Pavlov showed that a bell signalling that food is on the way can prompt the same conditioned response.

B. Frederick Skinner's work in the 1940s and 1950s gave added impetus to behaviourism. He pioneered "operant conditioning", a technique to relieve fear and anxiety by conditioning behaviour, which works by making the patient's behaviour a focus of reward and pleasure. For example, someone who fears going to a shopping centre may be encouraged to make repeated trips and be rewarded for doing so. Therapy may include keeping a diary and relaxation training.

Behaviour therapists maintain that by changing **behaviour,** they can change **thoughts** whereas **cognitive therapists** maintain that by changing **thoughts** they can change **behaviour**. They're both right. In fact, both kinds of therapy are practised in combination, to a greater or lesser degree. The terms "cognitive therapy" (CT) and "cognitive behaviour therapy"(CBT) are, in essence, interchangeable. There is also considerable overlap between CBT and psychoanalysis. Both require the client to report on their thoughts, feelings and wishes.

Ivan Petrovich Pavlov: Nobel prize-winner and pioneer of conditioned reflex research – the so-called "Pavlovian response." His ground-breaking work in the early 20th century prompted research into a wide range of emotional disorders. His discoveries still influence psychology research today.

How did CBT develop?

CBT, the most extensively researched psychological treatment for depression, was developed by the US psychiatrist Aaron Beck (1921–). He is the father of "the thinking man's psychotherapy", renowned for its strong scientific foundations and the basic humanity underpinning both its theory and practice. Beck believed that some people are vulnerable to depression because they develop negative or dysfunctional thoughts and feelings about themselves as a result of early learning experiences.

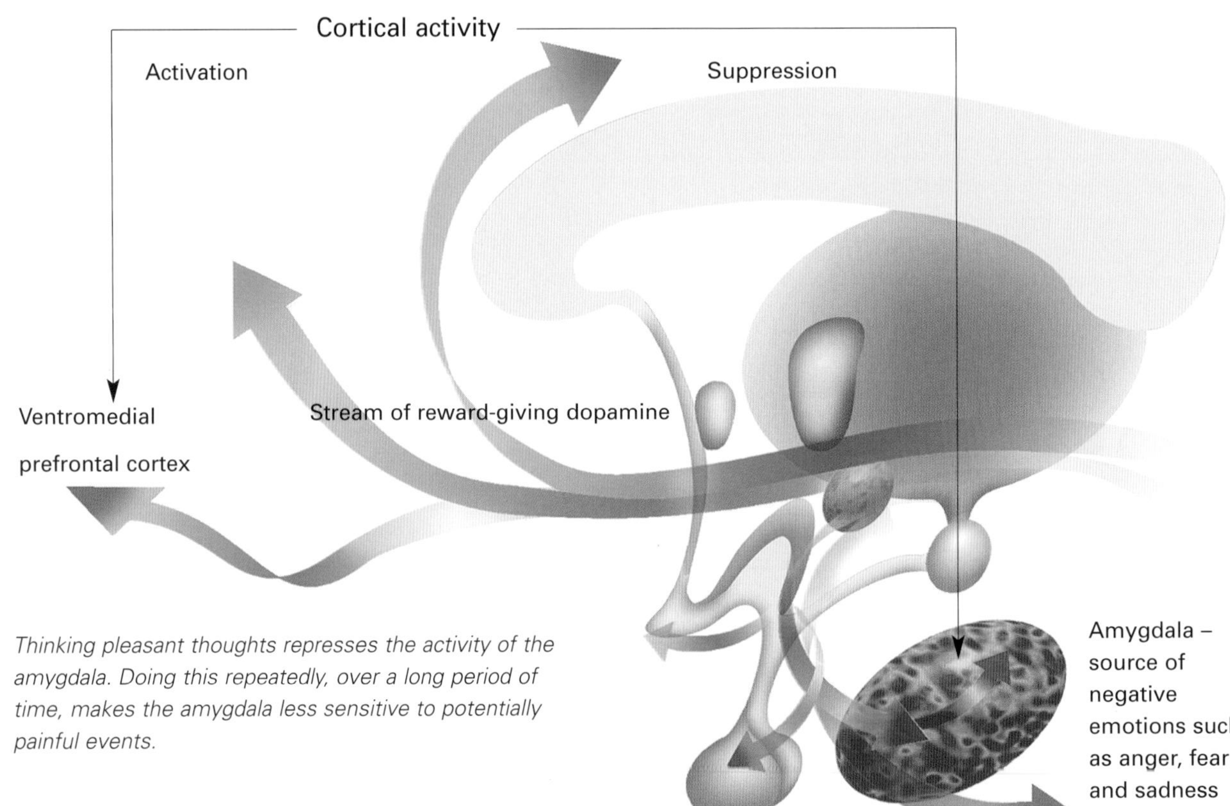

Thinking pleasant thoughts represses the activity of the amygdala. Doing this repeatedly, over a long period of time, makes the amygdala less sensitive to potentially painful events.

Early in life, Beck experienced feelings of abandonment, sadness, fear and anxiety about his health. He overcame a life-threatening illness and still finished one year ahead of his student peers. As a psychiatrist, he faced professional isolation and rejection when he abandoned psychoanalysis for cognitive therapy. He became disenchanted with "free association", an integral part of psychoanalysis, in which the patient is encouraged to report freely on their thoughts as they occur. The more his clients "free associated", he found, the worse they became. They tended to do better if he helped them understand practical problems. CBT assumes the key to many psychological difficulties lies not deep in the unconscious, but on the surface. One of Beck's favourite maxims is that there is more to the surface than meets the eye.

Working independently of Beck, the US psychologist Albert Ellis reached similar conclusions pioneering "rational emotive therapy" – the replacement of self-defeating thoughts with realistic, rational ones.

There are interesting similarities between Ellis and Beck: Ellis (1913–) developed a serious kidney disorder in childhood and turned from sports to books. His parents divorced when he was 12. As a psychoanalyst he found clients did as well when he saw them only once a week or even every other week instead of daily. He also abandoned passive psychoanalytic procedures for a more active role. Recalling how he had worked through his own problems by reading the philosophies of Epictetus, Marcus Aurelius and Bertrand Russell, he told clients what had helped him, encouraging them to challenge irrational beliefs about themselves.

Beck developed cognitive therapy to treat depression, but it is now used for a range of problems – including anxiety, anger management, obsessive compulsive disorder, shyness and even gambling.

Positive thoughts fire up neurons which produce the chemical dopamine in the brain (see illustration, left). This activates cortical areas in the brain, and in turn feeds back to the amygdala, suppressing neuronal firing there. The result is a positive feedback "loop" – the converse of the vicious circle of depression (see page 42), which moderates the negative activity of the amygdala. The more frequently, and intensely, the amygdala is activated by negative emotions – especially in infancy – the more likely it is to respond strongly in future to the slightest "bad" thing.

2 Understanding CBT

"There is nothing either good or bad,
but thinking makes it so."

William Shakespeare, *Hamlet*, Act 2, scene ii

How does CBT work?

As a first step towards understanding CBT, imagine trying to clear a fuzzy TV image. You want the *true* picture. CBT treats disorders in which people, in effect, lose sight of the true picture. Clinically depressed people feel bad about themselves – their self-image becomes fuzzy and distorted. CBT suggests that how we think largely determines how we feel. The focus of CBT is on thoughts, beliefs assumptions and perceptions – on everything affecting how we know and interpret the world.

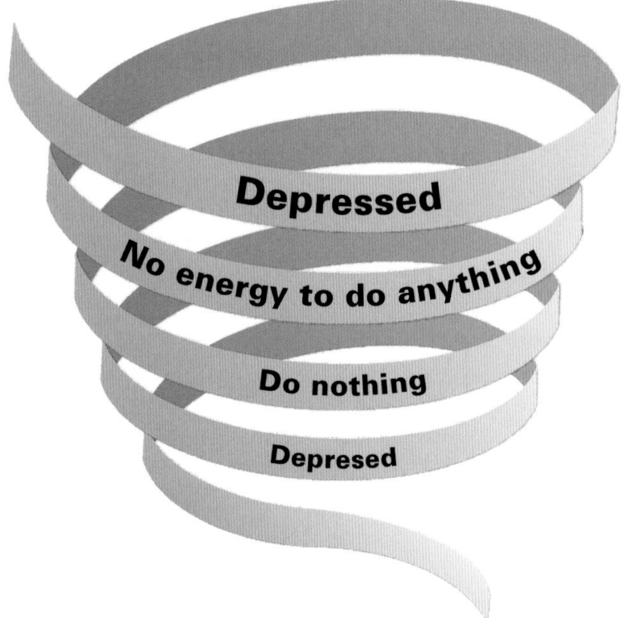

In depression, gloomy thoughts take over and we interpret things in a negative way (see opposite). These negative responses cause depressed thinking and feelings which can become self-perpetuating, leading to a vicious circle, locking you into depression. Think negatively and you'll begin to feel unhappy, sad or overwhelmed, and this may ultimately affect how you behave. You may stop seeing your friends or other things you enjoy – like gardening or cooking or going to the cinema. CBT aims to break this think-feel-behave cycle.

Many theorists, including Freud and the classical psychoanalysts, see people with emotional problems as victims who can exert little if any control over their feelings. Using the fuzzy picture analogy, it's as if they cannot clarify or correct the picture. In cognitive therapy, people with depression are seen as victims of skewed thinking who can correct "the picture". They just need to get to the controls to do so.

Changing attitudes

Situation	Negative responses	Positive responses
You telephone your boy-/girlfriend, but there's no reply	He's/she's probably gone off with another date	I hope he's/she's having a good day
You're praised for a good presentation, but your boss suggests areas where it could be even better	He wants to sack me	Those are great ideas that I can use in many different ways
You're giving a dinner party and you forget the avocado for the mixed salad	This will ruin the entire evening	Oh well, there's more than enough to eat
You fail one module in an exam, while passing nine others	I'm no good – a total failure	Having passed so many, I can still get the final one
You fall over in the street and smash a bottle on the pavement	Absolutely everything is going wrong	Things could have been so much worse – it might have been me that got broken

"People who are highly competent sometimes feel deeply inadequate: people who are inferior feel superior; people with an ordinary appearance feel beautiful; and people who are attractive feel ugly....Some people who have lived exemplary lives are torn with severe guilt to the point they no longer wish to live, while those who have committed horrendous crimes suffer not a twinge of conscience."

Ervin Straub, 'The Self-Concept: A Review and the Proposal of an Integrated Theory of Personality', in *Personality, Basic Aspects and Current Research*, Englewood Cliffs, Prentice Hall, 1980

What are the basic ideas behind CBT?

Beck's theory of depression includes three main components:

1. Negative automatic thoughts:

Thoughts or mental reflex actions which just "pop into the head" or "come out of the blue" without being in the forefront of our minds. We may automatically accept them even if they are distorted or irrational. One negative idea then amplifies another. Beck describes depression as "a cognitive triad": one component can reinforce the next:

- A negative view of the self ("I'm a failure")
- A negative view of the world ("This city is awful")
- A negative view of the future ("There are no prospects for me")

2. Depressive "schemata":

Any negative or dysfunctional thoughts and feelings we develop about ourselves early in life are reflected in schemata – the building blocks of cognition. Schemata are sets of attitudes or assumptions which shape our beliefs about others, ourselves and the world. We have schemata about everything and none are more important than those relating to "the self system": self-esteem, self-awareness, self-image, self-blame, etc.

Self-schemata develop over many years and become ingrained in our psyche from infancy. They may change throughout life, but the old ones never completely disappear, and may re-emerge as a result of stress, so while a young boy who's consistently told he's no good at essays may later become a prize-winning author, he may never completely shake off his early sense of inadequacy. His self-esteem could be highly vulnerable to one bad review, which would undo all the good work he had done on it.

Factors in childhood leading to depressive schemata

Tangible loss

- Loss of mother/father
- Loss of other relative, friend, person close to you (loss includes death, divorce, separation, desertion, prolonged ill-health)
- Prolonged ill-health as a child

Expectation of loss (reality)

- Loss of mother/father or other close person expected for long time before loss actually realized
- Disappointment by people relied upon
- Expectation of big reward for something done, which never materialized

Expectation of loss (fantasy)

- Loss (as in previous category) expected for a long time which does not actually occur

Reversal in valuation of object

- Sudden change from loving someone very much to hating them
- Sudden change from self-respect to self-hate – feeling badly about self because of an event

Self-esteem lowering events

- Difficulty in mixing with other children
- Being bullied over an extended period
- Feeling of being different from peer group
- Feeling of being unwanted by parents
- Feeling of being unwanted by everyone ("no one cared")
- Feeling of being hated by everyone

Background

- Depression in close family members
- Severe punishment by either parent
- Overprotection by either parent, and/or isolation from other children
- Strict rules by either parent
- History of parents pointing out faults but not good points

3. Logical errors in thinking

Beck described these categories:

Arbitrary inference: *A conclusion reached on the basis of insufficient evidence or no evidence at all.* For example, Harry becomes convinced he won't get his promotion because his taxi to the interview is late.

Selective abstraction: *A conclusion based on just one of many factors.* For example, Wendy is a good conference organizer. She runs a successful meeting, with many highlights including excellent speakers, good attendance and running to time, however, one speaker fails to turn up. She blames herself for the "failure" of the entire event.

Over-generalization: For example, an actor playing Hamlet wins critical acclaim, but berates himself for forgetting one line on the first night. The audience hardly notices, but he cannot forget this momentary lapse, and draws the false conclusion that he is a terrible actor.

Magnification: For example, James was a perfectionist who feared that his entire routine was going to fall apart because he had not jotted down a minor task in his diary.

Such errors of thinking can spark a cognitive chain reaction (see opposite).

"Beck's cognitive therapy has started to blossom and it is easy to see why. Unlike psychoanalysis its techniques are straightforward, easily described and deliberately free of mystique. Moreover, unlike behaviourism, cognitive therapy is explicitly human both in its origins and in its applications. Its rationale is based on reasoned arguments and the persuasive power of evidence. The thinking man's psychotherapy if you like."

Robert E. Kendall, *Cognitive Therapy for Depression and Anxiety (foreward)*, Ivy Marie Blackburn and Kate Davidson, Blackwell Science, 1995

The depressive chain reaction

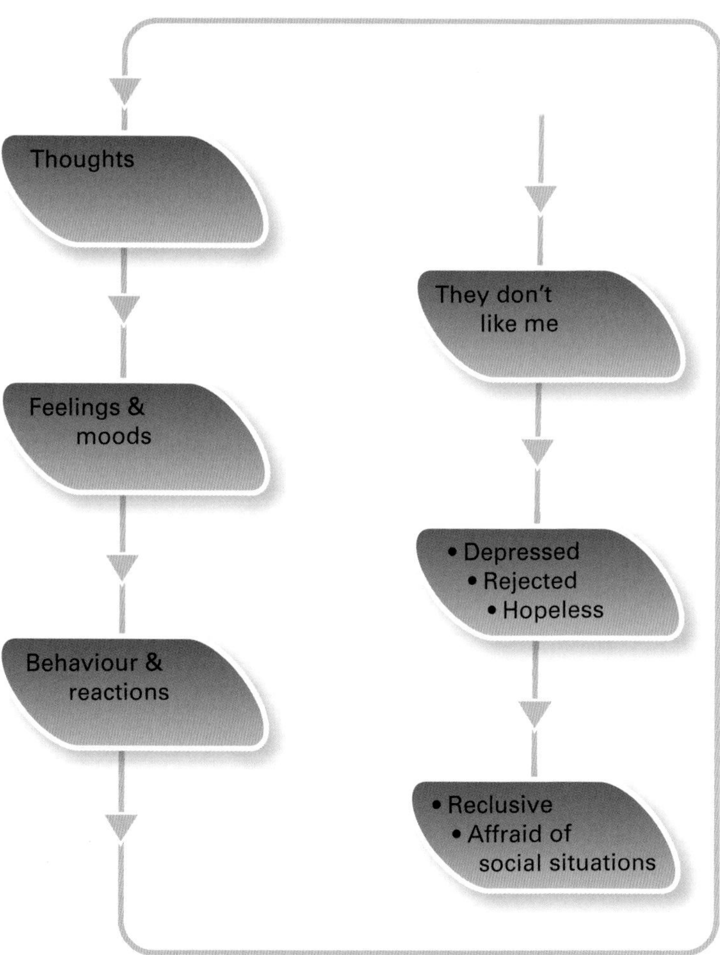

"People are disturbed not by things, but by the view they take of them."

Epictetus,
Greek philosopher

3 Approaches to treatment

"Compared to psychoanalysis, cognitive therapy certainly does appear much simpler, but we should not take this to mean that it is less profound. The central failure of the founders of psychoanalysis was that they did not recognize the true significance of thoughts in human neurosis. Once that significance was grasped by those like Aaron Beck, then human psychological disorders became more readily understandable and therefore simpler."

James Le Fanu, ***Overcoming Depression**: **A self help guide using Cognitive Behavioural Techniques (foreword)***, **Paul Gilbert, 1997**

What makes CBT different from other therapies?

Undergoing CBT is not like being a patient in the traditional sense. As a CBT patient, think of yourself less as a patient, and more as a scientist working in close collaboration with another scientist (your therapist) to identify and resolve a problem. Your "negative thought" becomes a scientific hypothesis or idea that is tested by collection and evaluation of data – just as in a scientific study.

This partnership approach is in line with one of the defining trends in modern healthcare. With the spread of healthcare information via the internet, the emergence of powerful patient advocacy groups and a general awareness of healthy living, the patient has ceased to be just a passive recipient. We have "the informed patient", the "expert patient" and "the doctor-patient partnership".

This cultural shift challenges a healthcare system traditionally characterized by paternalism and "the passive patient". The new phrase of the moment is "patient power". This is all very well if you're fit and healthy and going to the doctor for a check-up, but it's not easy to be a pro-active patient if, say, you have a newly diagnosed cancer. As previously noted, many a cancer patient has been grateful for an old fashioned slug of paternalism. Similarly, it's not easy to be pro-active if you have depression. CBT relies on the patient playing an active role and developing a collaborative relationship with the therapist. This can be hard work.

Putting theory into practice

Duration: A typical CBT programme may comprise 15–20 weekly sessions, perhaps twice weekly initially in the case of severe depression. A typical session lasts 50–60 minutes.

The session agenda: This is worked out at the start of each session and may take ten minutes or so. The therapist will ask what you want to discuss and set targets for the session.

Structure: Time will be allocated to specific issues. CBT tends to be highly structured to encourage a business-like, problem-solving approach – in contrast to the "free association" of psychoanalysis where the patient has free rein to talk about whatever comes to mind. The patient may do increasingly more of the agenda setting and structuring sessions as they get to know the routine.

Session target(s): Meeting targets is the major focus of each session. This may involve breaking down a particular problem into different components to see it in a new perspective. There is no magic formula. Different approaches work for different people. Working out what's best for you may involve trial and error.

Homework: A vital part of CBT: assignments may include "reality testing" (see page 114) and keeping a diary to monitor mood changes day by day (see page 119). Reviewing homework is a routine part of a session.

Feedback: The therapist may constantly seek feedback throughout the sessions to check if the patient feels things are going in the right direction. Feedback also reduces any chance of the patient not speaking out if a session – as can happen – makes them depressed or anxious. (Self-examination is not an easy process.)

What can I expect from my treatment?

There are many techniques used in CBT. Some are used for treatment sessions; some for homework assignments; some for both. Most are aimed at modifying negative or anxiety-provoking thoughts. The following are techniques which you may come across:

1. Examining the evidence for and against a negative thought

Harry's case ('Logical errors in thinking', page 106) highlights the basic treatment approach. In this example, his long wait for a taxi left him increasingly anxious about his job interview. Convincing himself that the taxi's late arrival meant he wasn't in the running for promotion, he was about to cancel the taxi when the driver finally knocked on the door.

The therapist set out to challenge Harry's negative belief by examining the evidence both for and against it:

- What was the evidence he wouldn't get the job?
- Was there another interpretation of the evidence?

The idea was to make Harry consider an alternative scenario and ask himself critical questions, such as:

- Why did I get an interview if I had no chance of getting the job?
- Was there any evidence I was less likely to be successful than anyone else?
- Was there any evidence I'd done a bad job?
- How did I get on with the boss?

He actually got on well with the boss and was the only person in his team to have consistently met the company targets over the previous 12 months. But he hadn't met *his own* personal targets – which, on reflection, he later realized, had been unrealistic. He realized that the evidence to support his negative thought just didn't stand up.

The therapist asked Harry to imagine waiting for the taxi again and posed questions which led to Harry asking:

- Was there anything wrong about feeling anxious in my situation? Wasn't it just a natural reaction?
- How did the other candidates feel before their interviews?
- Could I have done something more useful while waiting, instead of striding briskly up and down the kitchen repeatedly looking at my watch?

Harry could have phoned his boss to explain that the taxi was late, tried a simple relaxation technique, or worked out answers to possible questions in his interview. The session not only made Harry re-evaluate this particular thought process; it also made him examine other negative thought processes.

2. Reality testing

Tables are used in "reality testing" techniques – as in the case of Terry (see opposite). He repeatedly called his girlfriend without reply. His therapist encouraged him to test the validity of his negative thought (that Jackie had "gone off" him) by creating a reality chart which involved the following stages:

- **Identifying the notion/hypothesis and rating it in terms of belief (does he really believe it?) on a scale of one to a hundred.**
- **Working out what it could predict (i.e., the end of the relationship).**
- **Devising a homework project to test it out.**
- **Revaluating his method of data collection, as well as re-rating his original belief.**

His homework included collecting the evidence to test his fear (the hypothesis) that Jackie didn't want to go out with him anymore. This included talking to Jackie and, more importantly, assessing if there was any real evidence that might point towards his hypothesis. He could ask himself "Has she ever told me she's bored of me?" or "Would she be my girlfriend if she didn't want to be?". He might question whether he trusts her and hopefully the answer will be that yes he has had no reason not to trust her. Realizing his thinking had been "off-beam" encouraged him to think differently and "re-set" certain cognitive processes.

Rationalising responses

Thought-provoking event	Feelings	Negative thought	Rational response		Result
Phoning Jackie: no answer – repeatedly	Sad, depressed, concerned and anxious	She's gone off me She's bored with me She's gone off with someone else **Belief = 90%**	I'm sure she'll be back soon She's probably been delayed at work She's probably helping a friend or her mother. I hope she's OK	HOME WORK	Terry's re-evaluates his belief rating – giving it a zero "belief rating" **Belief = 0 %**

Terry collects the evidence (data) to test his fear (the hypothesis) that Jackie doesn't want to go out with him anymore. Using a grid helped him to see the gulf between his rational and irrational thoughts or feelings.

Of course there are times when a person's negative thoughts are justified. Other people's behaviour is not so easily modifiable, and should not be the focus of treatment. Another strategy would be needed and this could be the basis of more traditional counselling.

3. Success therapy / graded task assignments

Lack of energy in depressive illness can often lead to inactivity. "Success therapy" is designed to encourage routine activities such as going to work, cooking, going for a walk, going shopping, playing a game, watching TV or listening to the radio. Therapist and patient will agree targets for the week, graded according to how long each one may take and how hard it is. An initial "cooking target" may be something basic like boiling an egg or toasting a piece of bread. New targets are set as you achieve *success.* A therapist will probably challenge a patient who says "I can't do that", and seek evidence of their inability and ask them to compile an activity schedule (see opposite). Completing it may in itself encourage a patient to do more.

4. Activity scheduling

People usually find that when they engage in an activity their mood lifts. The problem with depression is that people stop doing things and their mood gets worse as a result. Activity scheduling seeks to reverse that process and enables you to log your progress over a period of days, weeks or months. Looking over your progress in black and white is surprisingly encouraging. Activity scheduling may involve Beck's concept of mastery and pleasure. The theory behind mastery and pleasure is, quite simply, that we all need to feel good about ourselves – and that we need to have this feeling *reinforced,* for example, by a compliment, or by passing an exam or by doing well on the sports field. Such accomplishments, or mastery can be rated on a ten-point scale. Pleasure, referring to pleasant, enjoyable feelings from a specific activity, could also be rated on a ten-point scale.

Example activity schedules

Pre-therapy activity schedule

		Mastery	Pleasure
7–8 am	Got up, dressed, breakfast	0	0
8–10 am	Sat in chair with newspaper	0	0
11–12 am	Dozed off	0	1
12–1 pm	Lunch	0	0
1–3 pm	Sat in front of TV	0	1
4–5 pm	Nothing recorded: "pointless"		
5–6 pm	Nothing recorded: "pointless"		
6–7 pm	Nothing recorded: "pointless"		
7–9 pm	Nothing recorded: "pointless"		

Post-therapy activity schedule (six months on)

		Mastery	Pleasure
7–8 am	Got up, got dressed, ate breakfast	3	4
8–10 am	Read newspaper	4	5
11–12 pm	Went for swim	5	9
12–1 pm	Had lunch	3	5
1–3 pm	Went shopping	5	8
4–5 pm	Drink with friend	4	9
5–6 pm	Prepared evening meal	3	4
6–7 pm	Ate with family	3	5
7–9 pm	Watched TV with husband	3	8

Using mastery and pleasure ratings can unlock the key to enjoyment – as in Anne's case (see the activity on the previous page). She had complained: "I just don't feel like a genuine person anymore. I can't seem to feel much at all. It's as if I'm not here." A 44-year-old housewife, she said she didn't deserve "to have fun". Her first activity schedule suggests her only pleasures were "dozing off" and "sitting in front of the TV" – even these things brought her only minimal enjoyment. Asked to rate her activities for the whole day, she stopped at 3pm, saying it was "pointless".

Seeking something she might enjoy and learning she had once been a keen swimmer, the therapist asked for her first thought about going swimming. She replied: "I have not got a swimming costume," – a small problem, but a typical barrier put up by a depressed patient who may find the most minor obstacle unsurpassable. Her homework assignment was to buy a swimming costume and go for a swim. She refused initially, but after additional treatment, she had her first swim for years – and went on to enjoy being in the pool.

Using a similar approach, she also increased her mastery and pleasure of other activities such as shopping. The post-therapy activity schedule shows significant improvements in her mastery and pleasure ratings – and a lifting of her depressed mood.

There are numerous resources available to help with activity scheduling. Some computer CBT packages, for example, provide charts and guidelines for scheduling and diaries.

5. Keeping a diary

This helps to log thoughts and feelings, and may involve "thought catching"– you monitor your feelings and "catch" the accompanying thoughts and record them in a "thought diary". This may pinpoint critical differences between absolute negative thoughts and rational responses to a particular event. For example, Ian recorded this entry:

- **Day:** Monday
- **Situation:** The telephone rings.
- **Emotions:** Immediate fear that it's the boss. Sense of weariness and despair. What does he want now? Sense of alarm and depressed feelings.
- **Automatic negative thoughts:** He's going to tell me off or give me a rocket.
- **Completion of homework:** Ian establishes by checking his e-mails that there is nothing that he has done wrong.
- **Rational response:** The boss must have forgotten due to his own workload when my sales report is due in. He might have to speak to me about a company-wide issue and is speaking to everyone in turn not just me.

Ian was convinced he was in trouble. His boss was on the phone, not to give him a rocket, but to thank him for doing such a good job. Ian reminded himself to assess the evidence for his fear and to give a rational response. Thinking things through, he realized his boss had good reason to be pleased with him. He'd been working hard and effectively.

A behaviour diary (see page 121) can establish the link between feelings (questions 1 and 2) and symptoms (questions 3 and 4) and behaviour (questions 5–7) and help you to achieve your "target behaviour", or goals.

Cognitive rehearsal, role play and "alternative" therapy

Negative thinking convinces people they can't do certain things. In cognitive rehearsal, they imagine themselves trying "the impossible". The therapist might take them through their thought processes step by step, asking: "What would you be thinking about at this time when faced with your particular problem?" This can help to identify mental blocks.

For example, Mary felt overwhelmed by work, but unable to tell her boss. She was anxious and depressed, both about her workload and her failure to stand up for herself. Role play in which she played herself talking to her boss encouraged her to confront him. She actually finished up handing in her notice and getting a better paid, less demanding job, but the immediate, surprising result was that her boss had told her that he actually felt guilty about her workload. He'd been powerless to do anything about it, he claimed. Her therapy included assertiveness training.

In "alternative therapy" the patient is asked to imagine an alternative to a depressing situation. Mary's alternative was to find a better paid, less demanding job. There may be several alternative solutions to a particular problem. For example, John became severely depressed while spending a week "home alone"– and considered taking an overdose. Possible alternatives included seeing more of his friends, going out more, seeing his GP, going shopping or getting out of the house more to go to the cinema and theatre. Alternative therapy seeks to encourage the patient to view their "alternatives" to being depressed, and help them see their alternatives as potential realities.

The following pages provide space for you to record your thoughts, feelings and reactions to activities you engage in. You and your therapist should decide between you which activities are most suitable for you to attempt if you are having difficulty getting motivated.

Behaviour diary

Name **Today's date**

How anxious/tense have you been today?

0 1 2 3 4 5 6 7 8 9 10

Not at all Moderately Extremely

How depressed have you been today?

0 1 2 3 4 5 6 7 8 9 10

Not at all Moderately Extremely

How has your appetite been today?

0 1 2 3 4 5 6 7 8 9 10

Very poor Moderate Very good

How did you sleep last night?

0 1 2 3 4 5 6 7 8 9 10

Very badly Moderately Very well

How long did you spend.............................. today?..

(or) How many times did you .... today?..

How did you cope with .... today?..%

How long did you spend.............................. today?..

(or) How many times did you .... today?..

How did you cope with.................................. today?..%

How long did you spend.............................. today?..

(or) How many times did you .... today?..

How did you cope with .... today?..%

Any other comments..

Thoughts and feelings diary

Time	Monday	Tuesday	Wednesday
7am– 8am			
8am– 9am			
9am– 10am			
10am– 11am			
11am– 12pm			
12pm– 1pm–			
1pm– 2pm–			
2pm– 3pm–			
3pm– 4pm–			
4pm– 6pm–			
6pm– 8pm–			

Thursday	Friday	Saturday	Sunday

4 Therapy options

"The cognitive approach is not merely 'positive thinking', which may be ineffective in the long term....Changes in thinking need to be genuine if they are to free an individual from distress. An individual's endeavour to think positively may simply mean that they try to deceive or trick themselves, and such self-deception would be unlikely to be sustainable."

Simon Easton, '*Psychological Health: Helping people in stress and distress*', from *Mind-Body Medicine: A Clinician's Guide to Psychoneuroimmunology*, **Dr Alan Watkins (ed), Churchill Livingstone, 1997**

How can I get CBT?

Getting a CBT therapist is not easy because of the shortage of trained therapists. For example, of the estimated seven million people in the UK alone who might benefit from psychotherapy for problems of anxiety and depression, just 70,000 do so, according to research.[1] The UK situation reflects an international problem.

This highlights the key role of self-help books like this and the emergence of computerized CBT. CBT self-help books used to provoke suspicion, but "bibliotherapy" (a book without any other therapy) has been shown to be as effective as conventional one-to-one therapy or anti-depressant drugs. Of course, it depends on the book – some self-help books are better than others. A self-help book may also be used successfully *in conjunction* with medication or formal psychotherapy.

Thus, self-help books and computer programmes are increasingly seen as an important extension to patient choice. As the contributors to a book on "tele-psychiatry" and e-mental health put it: "It is unlikely that there will ever be enough skilled therapists to meet all the needs of all those suffering from common mental health problems….We envisage a future in which only those patients who cannot be helped by self-help books or computer therapy programmes will need to call upon 'live' therapists".[2]

Of course, there will be *many* patients who need more than a book or more than a computer programme – and you should definitely see your doctor if you are depressed.

Can't I just curl up with a self-help book like this one?

Is there any evidence that self-help books can work? Yes: scientific research has proved conclusively that they have a genuine role to play in therapy. *The Feeling Good Handbook*, for example, has been subjected to extensive academic scrutiny. A bumper 732 pages, this highly acclaimed title encompasses everything from depression to anxiety; from fears to phobias; and from dealing with difficult people to intimate communication. Following up depressed patients three years after they had first used the handbook, independent researchers found that 70 per cent had not sought or received any further treatment with medication or psychotherapy during the follow-up period.

As the author, US psychiatrist David Burns, comments: no treatment is a cure-all. He says, "A 70 per cent success rate is similar to the improvement rates reported for antidepressant medications as well as cognitive behaviour therapy and for interpersonal therapy (see below). It is encouraging that so many patients seem to respond to self-help therapy alone, but it is also clear that patients with more severe or chronic depression need the help of a therapist and possibly an antidepressant medication as well. This is nothing to be ashamed of, different individuals respond better to different approaches."[3]

Interpersonal therapy is another short-term form of psychotherapy which focuses on the influence of relationships on depression. It is not as well established as CBT. Practitioners maintain that although depression may not be caused by interpersonal factors, it has almost inevitable interpersonal impact – in that it affects relationships and the roles within them. The first one to three sessions of interpersonal therapy are given over to identifying specific interpersonal issues. These then become the focus of the new therapy.

Human contact – key to effective therapy?

Surely human contact is critical – the starting point in treatment has always been the doctor–patient or therapist–client relationship. This is where using your brain comes into its own. Most people assume an effective "therapeutic relationship" has to be "real" – a traditional face-to-face meeting between two people, characterized by both non-verbal (body language) and verbal communication. In fact, psychotherapy is designed to *maximize* the verbal components of the relationship and *minimize* the non-verbal. There's no eye contact, no touch. Freud put his patients on the couch and sat behind them – a convention that continues – to *avoid* eye contact. We also know from bibliotherapy that human contact is not necessarily a prerequiste of successful therapy.

The new computer-based "client-software relationships" that are evolving via CBT computer programmes (CCBT) are likely to be even more controversial than self-help books, even though they have all the same potential benefits. Three researchers, Kate Cavanagh, David A. Shapiro and Jason S. Zack, summarized the pros and the cons of CCBT, which are presented clearly on the next pages for you to review.[4] (All these points apply equally to self-help books.)

Computer-based therapy – pros and cons

The pros include:

Less shame or embarrassment: Many people don't want to face another human being while recounting personal and distressing events or feelings.

Home comforts: People using their home computers can work at their own pace in a secure environment.

Waiting lists: CCBT is an alternative to waiting for months, even years, for a human therapist to become available.

Loss of stigma: The stigma associated with seeking help for depression may be reduced if patients are seen to be working to help themselves rather than "seeing a shrink".

Time saving: Home-based computer therapy may save money and time, bypassing the need to visit the therapist.

Cultural differences: People living in a culture other than their own may feel more comfortable in having access to help in their country of origin.

Disability: Home computer therapy may be better for disabled people who can't travel.

Colby and others noted other potential benefits (some of which also apply to books):[5]

- Computers are polite, friendly and always have good manners.
- Computer programmes do not get tired, bored or forgetful.
- Computer programmes never get irritated, annoyed or reproachful and will not show facial expressions of shock, contempt or surprise.
- Computers do not have family problems.
- Computers never get sick or hungover.
- Computers never try and sleep with the patient.

Moreover, unlike human therapists, who may vary in their approach between sessions and clients, psychotherapeutic software is consistent and can be updated.

The cons include:

Possible effects on traditional CBT: Some therapists fear CCBT might reinforce the unhelpful stereotype of CBT as lacking the human sensitivity of other forms of "talking therapies". (Others fear this viable and cheaper alternative might undermine traditional therapy.)

Consumer choice: Given the choice between traditional and CCBT therapy, it seems unlikely that many would opt for the latter.

Efficacy: It is impossible to predict which patients would benefit from CCBT. Here CCBT is no different from face to face or antidepressant therapy. Trial and error is a common feature of all depression therapy.

Technophobia: A significant problem, especially among older people. Here, of course, self-help books are not a problem.

Computer breakdown: Similarly, of course, books have the edge as they are user-friendly and don't behave unpredictably.

Are there any CBT computer programmes to treat depression?

You may not be offered CCBT unless you ask – and even then there's no guarantee. CCBT is very much in its infancy and most healthcare professionals are still unaware of it. See Part Three: Resources to find out more about the following programmes:

Good Days Ahead was developed in the US by Mindstreet, the original version and the first programme of its kind was designed for use primarily under clinical supervision. A self-help version for home use is now available. Professional actors portray characters overcoming anxiety and depression. For example, in one scenario, Joan, the main character, is visiting her friend Karen. She is shown having many distorted, automatic thoughts and the actors play out her rejecting her friend's offer of help. But then we see CBT techniques helping Joan to change her thinking.

Restoring the balance: A self-help programme for managing anxiety and depression is available from the UK Mental Health Foundation. It was developed for either doctors' surgeries or clinics, where therapist support is available, or as a DIY treatment for "well-motivated" users.

Beating the Blues is an eight-session programme developed for GP surgeries and mental health clinics; it features fictional case studies of depressed and anxious patients. Andrew, a teacher in his mid-twenties, feels overwhelmed and depressed. Elaine is a single parent with two children and serious money problems. Jean, a widow in her seventies, has become depressed after the death of a close friend. In a study of 170 patients[6] this programme was found to significantly reduce both anxiety and depression. It has been used in more than 60 UK centres.

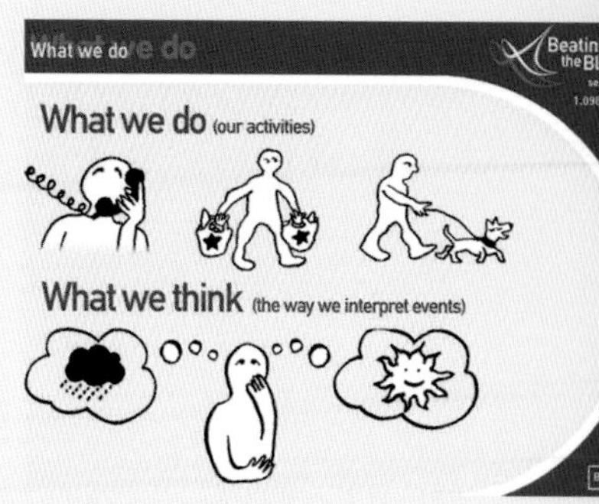

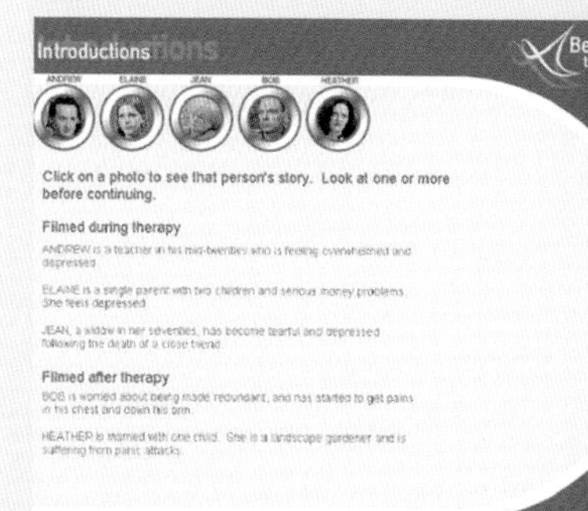

How easy is it to interact with a soulless computer?

Some people ask how a computer can be as warm and friendly as we'd like a human therapist to be. They're afraid to log on and confront their problems alone. This is why there's a big emphasis on making CCBT user-friendly – with lots of self-help exercises, quizzes, multiple choice questionnaires and case histories. It may or may not work for you – but there's conclusive evidence that it works for lots of people. It doesn't give you direct access to a therapist which may be helpful if you're feeling really low.

With this in mind *Beating the Blues* includes a "safety net" to monitor the patient's thoughts. The patient's doctor gets a brief weekly progress report from *Beating the Blues* about anxiety and depression ratings, how depressing their problems have been and whether they've had any upsets or suicidal thoughts. *Good Days Ahead* emphasizes that it's not a substitute for professional diagnosis and treatment and advises anyone with significant depression or anxiety to consult a doctor or therapist immediately if they have any suicidal thoughts.

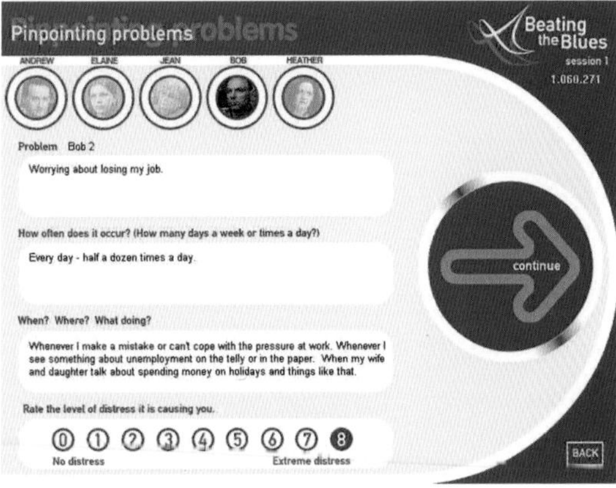

Susan's story

Susan, 50, married to a doctor, had a lifelong history of fluctuating mood and felt she hadn't fulfilled her potential. She felt fairly hopeless about her prospects, avoided social situations and felt "on the edge of an abyss". She'd taken antidepressants for three years without lasting effect and tried counselling, only to feel she should have made better use of it.

She tried *Beating the Blues* because she faced a long wait for a human therapist at a critical time and because she could work independently and was highly motivated. Being computer literate gave her confidence, but this is not a prerequisite for treatment.

Susan identified her therapy goals as being:

- To deal with minor problems without feeling desperate (which fitted in well with her view of herself as being pretty useless at things).
- To be more positive and look forward to life and feel more energized (which also fitted in well with her self-image).

CCBT taught her how to change her thoughts and focus on her strengths, which helped to motivate her and get her going. She stayed the course and completed all the homework. After eight sessions she no longer felt defeated by things, was increasingly sociable, and hopeful about the future. She enrolled on an internet website design course – something she'd put off for a year.

What did the human therapists responsible for Susan feel about using CCBT for the first time? One of them explained: "We have had to resolve various dilemmas, including the notion of our work being carried out by a machine.... We need to be mindful of the fact that just as there is no 'best therapy', there is equally no "best" means of delivering therapy.

5 CBT success rates

"Evidence that cognitive therapy works is persuasive. It is as effective as drug treatment in moderately severe depression and the effects may be more lasting. Combining the two may be the best option."

Professor Brice Pitt, ***Down with GLOOM or How to Defeat Depression*****, Gaskell, 1993**

What are the success rates of CBT? How does it compare with drugs?

The biggest challenge in treating depression is in finding a lasting successful treatment. This is not as easy as it sounds because any treatment can have a so-called "placebo effect" and work simply because we expect it to – a case of mind over matter.

This is why "placebo controlled" studies are used to test new medicines. In double blind studies, neither patients nor doctors nor nurses know which patients are receiving the placebo and which the real medicine. Placebo pills have been shown to have a strong therapeutic effect on patients with depression. Some studies have even concluded that antidepressants may not be much more effective than placebos. But in most cases this beneficial placebo effect doesn't last.

Relapse rates of patients taking "maintenance medication" have also been shown to be high. In 2003, The National Institute for Clinical Excellence in the UK reported that as few as 20 per cent of patients taking antidepressants recover and subsequently stay well for 18 months.[7]

CBT seems to increase the time patients remain well. Blackburn and Davidson have reported on six studies showing a marked improvement in relapse rates over a period of one or two years in patients treated with CBT alone, or in combination with drugs, compared with patients treated with drugs alone.[8] For example, in one study, the relapse rate for cognitive therapy alone after two years was 23 per cent; for the combined treatment 21 per cent; and for medication alone 78 per cent. In other words, the cognitive therapy patients were much less likely to relapse than the patients treated with drugs alone.

CBT – the facts

- CBT works as well as antidepressants in the treatment of depression of varying severity and it may be more effective in the long term, i.e. in preventing relapse.
- Combining drugs and CBT is more effective than using CBT alone.
- CBT alone sometimes works better than drugs alone.

What gives CBT the statistical edge? Blackburn and Davidson comment: "As cognitive therapy aims to teach coping skills, and is particularly focused on the attitudes and thinking style which are deemed to maintain depression, it is possible that patients can apply this learning at the beginning of a recurrence of depression, and hence prevent a full episode of depression from occurring. Another possibility is that the changes made during therapy bring about a permanent shift in a patient's cognitive style."

Statistics tell only part of the story and some patients are more likely to do well on CBT than others. In one study researchers gave patients starting treatment a book describing "the cognitive model" and how cognitive treatment works.[9] Patients who reacted favourably to the book were found to have done better after 12 weeks of therapy. Patients with an active rather than a passive style of coping are also more likely to benefit from CBT.

What are the potential problems with CBT?

Blackburn and Davidson have identified the following:

Homework: Some patients are not used to writing and feel shy or embarrassed from lack of practice or fear of spelling mistakes. They may also think their thoughts are too silly to write down. (See the case history opposite.)

"The patient who does not think": Some patients insist no thought goes through their mind when they feel depressed or anxious. The emotion just overcomes them out of the blue. Training can help to identify the "automatic thoughts" underlying their feelings.

"The patient who does not feel": Some patients "intellectualize" their problems, describing them in great detail, without taking into account their or other peoples' feelings. They may block emotions, believing that expressing them is "weak" or "unmanly", or that they're "trivial". The therapist may resolve this problem by interrupting the patient's flow repeatedly and asking: "What were you *feeling* at that time?"

The patient "who knows it all" and "recovers" in one treatment session: Some patients claim they "don't need any more therapy" and have been "feeling fine all week". They may be ashamed about needing help and fear for their privacy.

The patient who is reluctant to stop treatment: The patient becomes dependent on the therapist. This problem can be overcome by offering follow-up appointments at increasing intervals.[10]

CASE HISTORY:

Homework

During my first CBT session, my therapist said there would be about 30–45 minutes homework a day. My initial reaction was that as I found time for *Eastenders* and *The Simpsons* most days, it wouldn't be too big a problem to make time for something that was really going to benefit me. The assignments included concentration exercises and keeping a diary.

However, CBT homework is a bit like school homework. It takes effort and you'd probably much rather be doing something else. I had a diary I was meant to fill in at certain times. I gave up after two weeks, not because I didn't have enough time – you can always find the time if you really want to –- but because I lost the initial impetus and drive.

I quickly realized that without the diary, my sessions became less meaningful. Instead of describing exact emotional states, as one can if it's all written down at the time, I was referring to slightly hazy memories from a few days ago.

I found it hard to remember exactly how I felt a few hours later, let alone a few days later, so I re-started the diary, and it became a crucial reference point for me. But nonetheless I found it hard to honestly assess my situation. Your therapist can only know what he or she has been told. It's very easy to say that keeping secrets from your therapist will be detrimental to your therapy, but if you can't admit something to yourself, how can you admit it to someone else, even if they're trying to help you? Writing things down helped me to face up to myself in a way that I might not have done otherwise.

This is something demanding both bravery and perseverance. Bravery and perseverance are the key to the success of CBT.

David Charles, 25

Counselling or CBT – what's the difference?

You may well be offered counselling if you ask your doctor about CBT because there are many more counsellors than CBT therapists. For example, between 1992 and 1998, the number of doctor's surgeries in the UK offering counselling is reported to have risen from just under a third (31 per cent) to just over half. Counselling and psychotherapy developed separately, but the boundaries between them have become increasingly blurred over time.

"Counselling" has become almost synonymous with so-called "non-directive counselling". Developed by Carl Rogers in the 1940s, it is so called because he believed that people benefit more from having the confidence to resolve their problems rather than being told what to do or think. Counselling focuses on a specific problem, such as depression or a crisis, with a view to encouraging people to unlock their own inner resources.

Critics claim that counselling ignores underlying problems, but an analysis of six UK studies involving 772 patients found that counselling by a BACP accredited counsellor was more effective than usual GP care in reducing symptoms of depression and anxiety in the short-term (one to six months).[11] More than a third of the patients in the counselling group were significantly better after four months, compared with less than a quarter of those on standard GP care. However, counselling seemed no better than usual care in improving symptoms in the long term (beyond six months) nor in improving social function. By way of contrast, research suggests that CBT is the better bet.

Is it appropriate to compare drugs and counselling?

The Mental Health Foundation report, *Knowing our own minds,*[11] says that such a comparison may be inappropriate because people's expectations of the two forms of treatment are quite different. The perceived benefits of talking treatments (being listened to, being understood, gaining insight etc.) are not what people find helpful about medication.

It adds: "People tend to expect the relief of symptoms, an alteration of mood, even the disappearance of the original mental health problems from taking medication. Whereas, at their most helpful, talking treatments do what medication cannot do: provide someone with the opportunity to talk about their mental health problems within the context of their whole lives, validating their experiences, thoughts and feelings. In short, talking treatments have the capacity to attend to the self, to treat and respect the individual as a whole person in their own right."

This is not to say that CBT or counselling or any other form of talking treatment is invariably better than drugs. CBT may be too much for some people who may do better with supportive counselling – and no homework. Drugs alone will be the best option for others. Others will fare best using CBT and drugs. Again, this underlines the importance of becoming an expert patient. You should know what type of therapy you're being offered and what to expect, and what to do if it doesn't feel right.

Unfortunately, much antidepressant prescribing is inappropriate. More than 80 per cent of GPs in a British survey, published in March 2004, openly admitted over-prescribing antidepressants for "mild to moderate mental health conditions" because of the lack of psychological therapies. The survey, reflecting a European wide problem, was commissioned by Norwich Union Healthcare, and carried out by independent medical research specialists Dr Foster.

Choosing a therapist

The further information section (page 168) gives information on how to find a therapist. It may help to seek answers to these questions before starting any private treatment:

- What are your qualifications – are you fully qualified?
- What professional associations do you belong to?
- How much do you charge?
- How do you like to be paid – cheque or cash?
- How long have you been practicing?
- What areas do you specialize in?
- Where do you practice?
- Will what I say be confidential?*
- Do you subscribe to a particular code of ethics?
- How long is the treatment likely to take?
- What happens if I feel I'm making no progress after, say, three or four sessions?
- How often will we see one another?
- Will it be OK if I call between sessions – will you charge for this?
- What about any charges for cancelled appointments and holidays?

*Establish if the therapist will be discussing your case with a supervisor or any other third party.

"While you are hoping that the therapist is going to be able to help you, you are also about to help them pay part of their mortgage.... Remember that counsellors are in business....Counsellors should provide clear contracting and should make it clear what their qualifications are. We know of one or two cases where barely trained practitioners have set up in private practice and have not necessarily announced their, shall we say, lack of experience."

Windy Dryden and Colin Feltham, *Counselling and Psychotherapy: A Consumer's Guide*, Sheldon Press, 1995

Notes

Use this page to take down important information when considering a therapist. You can consult the guide (opposite) for a quick reminder of questions you should ask at an initial appointment, in a letter or over the phone.

6 The final story

"By far the greatest number of people who go through even the severest depression survive it, and live ever afterward at least as happily as their unaffected counterparts. Save for the awfulnes of certain memories it leaves, acute depression inflicts few permanent wounds....It is of great importance that those suffering a siege, perhaps for the first time, be told – be convinced, rather – that the illness will run its course, and that they will pull through."

William Styron, *Darkness Visible: A Memoir of Madness*, Vintage Books,1992

The final story

If current trends continue, the World Health Organization has warned that by 2020 major depression will be second only to heart disease as a cause of disability – ahead of infectious diseases, cancer and accidents. This book is a response to that alarm call.

At present clinical depression is an underground illness, with up to 50 per cent of sufferers undiagnosed, according to one estimate.[1] Many are afraid to seek help because depression still carries a stigma and is seen as a sign of psychological weakness. In fact, depression is as much a physical illness as heart disease or cancer – and most patients (75–85 per cent) will respond to treatment if it is of the right type and is given in the right way. In the US, The American Psychiatric Association claims that 80–90 per cent of patients experience "significant improvement".

But treatments frequently fail. The benefits often do not last. Estimates from clinical trials of antidepressant drugs in the UK suggest that among people who are treated by their GP (rather than by a consultant psychiatrist) as few as one in five (20 per cent) of individuals recover and subsequently maintain improvement for 18 months after drug therapy.[2] Many patients stop treatment within weeks. This may go some way towards explaining claims that antidepressants are not much better than placebos or dummy treatments. Many patients stop antidepressants because of side effects without realizing that there may be a simple solution, such as lowering the dose or trying an alternative drug. Successful treatment is all about trial and error. In addition, it should be about providing the best possible treatment on the basis of "evidence-based medicine". Unfortunately evidence based medicine is conspicuous by its absence in the treatment of depression.

For mild to moderate depression, cognitive behaviour therapy (CBT) has been shown to be as effective and fast acting as antidepressants. Moreover, people treated with CBT are more likely to remain free of depression for longer than those treated with drugs alone. Combining CBT and drugs can produce an even bigger therapeutic response. In hospital outpatients, for example, the combination of cognitive therapy and medication was found to be superior to either treatment alone.[3]

How many people know about CBT, though? I live in a prosperous area in north London where people regard themselves as well informed. I asked 20 local supermarket shoppers if they knew about CBT. They had all heard of antidepressants, of course, but eleven knew absolutely nothing about CBT. Only three knew it was used to treat depression and anxiety. The remaining six had heard of CBT, but did not know it was used to treat emotional disorders. This was a very unscientific straw poll, but I suspect that my finding is representative of people all over the world.

Of course, drugs and CBT cannot work miracles. If a person's life is fundamentally unsatisfactory due to, say, a faltering partnership or severe financial problems, their vulnerability to depression is likely to remain until these things are sorted out. This book is not about these things, however. Its purpose is to alert people to, and explain more about, the treatments that work from the inside. Drugs and CBT alter a person's mood and thinking which may be a satisfactory "result" in itself. Alternatively they can help restore the clear-sightedness, energy and motivation a person needs to make life-changes that will prevent a future lapse into misery.

The holistic approach

Are exercise and diet natural antidepressants? It's a lovely idea, and some studies have found that regular exercise may be just as effective to treat mild to moderate depression as drugs. But an analysis of 14 studies in the *British Medical Journal* found that much of the research was flawed, and concluded that exercise should not replace standard depression treatment – especially in severe illness.

But the report also stressed the benefit of exercise. This is not as contradictory as it may sound. Exercise does have other health benefits and these may have a knock-on effect on mood. A sedentary lifestyle increases the risk of depression, while depression increases the risk of a sedentary lifestyle. In turn, being a "couch potato" can increase the risk of heart disease, which can increases the risk of depression.

Thus exercise may add an additional dimension to standard treatment. The UK Department of Health recommends at least 30 minutes of physical activity for adults on five or more days a week. This should be of at least a moderate intensity – similar to brisk walking – and can be taken in 10–15 minute bouts throughout the day.

There is a widespread assumption that diet affects mood. Undoubtedly it does in that sensible eating helps create or maintain good health, without which people are more likely to suffer mood disorders. Certain dietary deficiencies – of the 'B' vitamins, for example, have been linked with depression, and so have both low-fat diets (below 25% fat intake) and diets containing high quantities of saturated fats (generally, those that are hard at room temperature, such as butter and other animal fats). Alcohol, sugar and caffeine may give a short-term lift, but tend in the long-term to make depression and anxiety worse rather than better.

High carbohydrate diets are sometimes recommended for people with depression, on the speculative basis that carbohydrates act on the brain in a similar way to serotonin. However, the evidence for specific "antidepressant foods" is scant. To date only one type of nutrient – omega-3 fatty acids which are found mainly in oily fish, and some nuts and seeds – has been consistently reported to help combat low mood.

Holistic approaches to treating mental disorders are starting to attract scientific study and in time, perhaps, a proven "antidepressant lifestyle" may emerge. For the moment, though, the most that can be said with certainty is that the chances of a full recovery from depression are enhanced if the person can maintain a generally healthy regime.

Eating an adequate and balanced diet: This means including all the major food groups: complex carbohydrates (staples such as rice, cereals, bread, pasta), protein (from meat, fish, nuts, poultry), fats (mainly unsaturated oils) and plenty of fresh fruit and vegetables (five or more portions a day). Go easy on alcohol and caffeine, and avoid "junk food" high in sugar and saturated fat.

Sleeping sufficiently: But not too much. Most people do best on 7–8 hours sleep nightly. Bizarre as it may seem, a single short bout of sleep deprivation (3 hours or less sleep within a 24-hour period) can sometimes produce an astonishing lift of mood for a short period thereafter, and is worth trying if you know you have a couple of days when you know you will not have to drive, or operate machinery, or do anything else that requires sustained concentration. It is not a long-term solution, however, and you should not attempt to deprive yourself of sleep for more than two nights in a row.

Exercise: If the prospect of half an hour's daily exercise seems daunting, begin with just a few minutes and slowly increase the amount you do each day. Make sure you exert yourself enough to increase your heart rate at least slightly above normal, and try to do it in the fresh air and, ideally, in varying surroundings.

Relaxation: Regular meditation, yoga, aromatherapy and massage help to promote a feeling of wellbeing and can be helpful for depression, especially if it is associated with agitation and anxiety.

Part Three
Resources

Notes to the text

Part One

1 Spike Milligan and Anthony Clare, *Depression and How To Survive It.*

2 Association of the British Pharmaceutical Industry, *Target Depression*, 1999.

3 Tkachev D., Mimmack M., Ryan M.M., Wayland M., Freeman T., Jones P., Starkey, M., Webster M.J., Yolken R.H. and Bahn S,. 'Olgodendrocyte Dysfunction in schizophrenia and bipolar disorder', *The Lancet* 2003; 362: 798.

4 Heather Welford, *Feelings after Birth.*

5 Spike Milligan and Anthony Clare, *Depression and How To Survive It.*

6 Quoted (page 3) in *Essential Psychopharmacology of Depression and Bipolar Disorder*, Stephen M. Stahl.

7 Kesller R.C., Nelson C.B., McGonagle K.A., Liu J., Swartz M., Blazer D.G., 'Comorbidity of DSM-111 – major depressive disorder in the general population: results from the US National Comorbidity Survey', *British Journal of Psychiatry* 168; 168 (suppl 30): 17-30.

8 Holmes T. and Rahe R. 'The Social Readjustment Rating Scale', *Journal of Psychosomatic Research* l967; 2: 214.

9 Eisenberger N. and Liedberman M., 'Does Rejection Hurt? an fMRI study of Social Exclusion', *Science* 2003; 302. 5643. 290.

10 Association of the British Pharmaceutical Industry, *Target Depression*, 1999.

11 Tim Cantopher., *Depressive Illness: The Curse of the Strong.*

12 Reported in *Fresher Pressure*, Aidan Macfarlane and Ann McPherson.

13 Brice Pitt, *Down with Gloom.*

14 Bridges K.W., Goldberg D.P. 'Somatic presentation of DSM 111 psychiatric disorders in primary care'. *Journal of Psychosomatic Research* 1985; 29:563–9. Cited by M. Sharpe and S. Wessely in "Non-specific ill health: a mind-body approach to functional somatic symptoms" (p.171), *Mind-Body Medicine: a Clinician's Guide to Psychoneuroimmunology*, Edited by Alan Watkins.

15 Kelly D. and France R., *A Practical Handbook for the Treatment of Depression*, Parthenon Publishing Group, 1987.

16 National Institutes of Health press release re. three day consensus development conference, sponsored by the National Institute of Mental Health, the National Institute of Ageing and the NIH Office of Medical Applications of Research, 1991.

17 Marcus S., Flynn H., Blow F.C., Barry K.L., 'Depressive symptoms among pregnant women screened in obstetric settings', *Journal of Women's Health* 2003; 12: 4 (May).

18 Roth J., Schulkin J., Loewenstein G., 'To feel it is to treat it. The effects of obstetrician–gynecologists' personal experiences with depression upon their treatment of depressed patients.' Personal communication: G.L. and J.I.

19 Taylor D., Paton C., and Kerwin R. *The Maudsley: The South and Maudsley NHS Trust 2003 Prescribing Guidelines* (7th edition), Martin Dunitz, 2003.

20 Morrison A.L., *A User's Guide for Patients and Families, The Antidepressant Sourcebook.*

21 GP survey supported by PRiMHE (Primary Care Mental Health Education), reported by the UK Depression Alliance, 2003, Anderson I.M. et al., 'Evidence-based guidelines for treating depressive disorders with antidepressants: a revision of the 1993 British Association for Psychopharmacology guidelines.' On behalf of the Consensus Meeting, endorsed by the British Association for Psychopharmacology. *Journal of Psychopharmacology* 2000; 14(1):3–20.

22 Taylor D., Young C., 'Health authority adherence to prescribing related requirements of the National Service Framework for Mental Health', *Pharmaceutical Journal.* 267: 753–754.

23 Lacey R., *The Complete Guide to Psychiatric Drugs*: A Layman's Handbook, Ebury Press, 1991.

24 Andrew Morrison, A.L., *A User's Guide for Patients and Families, The Antidepressant Sourcebook.*

25 Montejo-Gonzalez A.L., Llorca G., Izquierdo J.A., Ledesma A., Bousono M., Calcedo A. *et al.* 'SSRI induced sexual dysfunction: fluoxetine, paroxetine, sertraline and fluvoxamine in a prospective multicenter, and descriptive clinical study of 344 patients.' *Journal of Sex and Marital Therapy* 1997; 23:176–94.

26 Phillips R.L., Slaughter J.R., 'Depression and Sexual Desire', *American Family Physician* 2000; 62: 782–6.

27 Barnes T., with The Samaritans, *Dealing with Depression*, Vermillion 1996.

28 Recommendation in *British National Formulary* No. 46; September 2003.

29 Taylor D., Paton C., and Kerwin R. *The Maudsley: The South and Maudsley NHS Trust 2003 Prescribing Guidelines* (7th edition), Martin Dunitz, 2003.

Part Two

1 Lovell, K and Richards, D., 'Multiple access points and levels of entry (MAPLE): ensuring choice, accessibility and equity for CBT services,' *Behavioural and Cognitive Psychotherapy* 2000; 28: 379–92.

2 Cavanagh, K. Zack, J. and Shapiro D. 'Empirically Supported Computerized Psychotherapy', *Telepsychiatry and e-Mental Health*, edited by Wootton R, Yellowlees P., and McLaren P., Royal Society of Medicine Press, 2003.

3 Burns D, *The Feeling Good Handbook*, Plume, 1999.

4 Cavanagh K., Zack, J. and Shapiro, D. 'The computer plays therapist: the challenges and opportunities of psychotherapeutic software'. *Technology and Counselling in Psychotherapy. A Practitioner's Guide*, edited by Stephen Goss and Kate Anthony, Palgrave Macmillan, 2003.

5 Colby K.M., Faught W.S. and Parkinson, R.C., 'Cognitive therapy of paranoid conditions: Heuristic suggestions based on a computer simulation model,' *Cognitive Therapy and Research*, 3:55–60.

6 Proudfoot J., Goldberg D., Mann A., Everitt B., Marks I., and Gray J., 'Computerized ,interactive, multimedia, cognitive behavioural programme for anxiety and depression in general practice,' *Psychological Medicine* 2003; 33(2): 217–27.

7 National Institute for Clinical Excellence, 'Guidance on the use of computerized cognitive behavioural therapy for anxiety and depression', *Technology Appraisal Guide* – No. 51. 2002.

8 Blackburn I., and Davidson K., *Cognitive Therapy For Depression and Anxiety*, Blackwell Science, 1995.

9 Fennell M. J. V., and Teasdale J. D., Cognitive Therapy for depression: individual differences and the process of change, *Cognitive Therapy and Research*, 1987; 11: 253–72.

10 Bower P., Rowland N., Mellor Clark J., Heywood P., Godfrey C., Hardy R., 'Effect-iveness and cost effective-ness of counselling in primary care', *Cochrane Review* 2003; The Cochrane Library, Issue 4.

11 Blackburn I., and Davidson K., *Cognitive Therapy For Depression and Anxiety*, Blackwell Science, 1995.

12 Mental Health Foundation report, 'Knowing our own minds: a survey of how people in emotional distress take control of their own lives'. 1997.

Conclusion

1 National Institute for Clinical Excellence, UK, Guidance on the use of computerized behavioural therapy for anxiety and depression. *Technology Appraisal Guidance* No. 51, October 2002.

2 Ibid

3 Blackburn I.M., Bishop S., Glen A.I.M., Whalley L.J., Christie J.E., 'The efficacy of cognitive therapy in depression: a treatment trial using cognitive therapy and pharmacotherapy, each alone and in combination,' *British Journal of Psychiatry* 1981; 139: 181–9.

Drug directory

This section includes a directory of antidepressants and a checklist of questions to discuss with your doctor. One of the most frequently asked questions is: how long will I have to take antidepressants for? We have already addressed the problem of patients coming off their drugs too quickly once they have started working and it can take up to two to four weeks or more for an antidepressant to start working properly. Responses do vary from patient to patient and a partial response may occur within a few days. You should consult the below purely in tandem with advice on antidepressant therapy given by your doctor.

There are three main phases of treatment your doctor may refer to:

- An initial acute treatment phase
- A continuation phase (recommended for all patients)
- A maintenance phase (for patients with recurrent severe depression).

The acute phase covers the first weeks of treatment until you achieve at least a 40–60 per cent improvement in symptoms. US research found that patients showing no clinical improvement after four weeks of treatment do not benefit from continuing the drug, but that continuing until six weeks is worthwhile in patients showing even modest improvement.[1] In view of the lower doses used in the UK, *The Drug and Therapeutic Bulletin* has advised that an initial trial of six to eight weeks is probably justified, with an increase in dose for patients who have modest improvement.[2] If the drug doesn't work, the patient can try another. This underlines a key message: that successful treatment involves trial and error. Don't assume on the basis of one (or more) failures that antidepressants will not help.

The continuation phase covers a period of four to six months full recovery, or about a year in elderly patients with normal mood and functioning, comparable to that before the depression began. You should continue the treatment throughout this period. An important point is: *incomplete recovery is the most important "risk factor" for relapse (recurrence of symptoms) within one year of stopping antidepressants.* Many patients stop treatment prematurely, believing themselves to be cured. *Feeling better is a sign that the treatment is working; it is not an indication that the patient is cured.*

Maintenance therapy covers periods – in severe cases a life-time – in which people who have recurrent depression take antidepressants to keep symptoms under control. Many people do not like the idea of maintenance therapy, but the counter-argument is that maintenance therapy is routinely used to treat heart disease, high blood pressure and asthma. Why not depression?

Finally, it is important to recognize the high number of treatment failures: *about 30 per cent of patients remain depressed despite initial antidepressant therapy.*[3] By recognizing what can go wrong you can give yourself the best possible chance of success. In other words, use your brain (and this book!) to help yourself.

The 30 per cent failure rate cited above is higher than some other estimates. Another estimate put the figure at between 10 and 20 per cent. Whatever the true figure, it is high.

What's in a name?

The directory that follows lists generic (chemical) and brand names of drugs. The generic name is the name of the active chemical ingredient of the drug and is usually longer than the brand name. For example, Prozac is the brand name for fluoxetine. The pharmaceutical industry is fiercely competitive and drug companies devote a lot of effort in choosing snappy sounding brand names for their products. The idea is to produce names that doctors will remember when they are writing prescriptions. Different brand names may contain the same active ingredient. Generic versions of drugs are just as effective as brands and usually cheaper – so doctors are encouraged to prescribe them. We found some brand names listed in the *British National Formulary* have been discontinued in the UK. For example, Elaviril (a brand name for amitriptyline) was not available from DDSA Pharmaceuticals Ltd.), but it is available in other countries.

Drug checklist

Important questions to ask your doctor before you start a course of drug treatment:

- What's the name of the drug I am being prescribed?
- What's it for?
- Will it interact with any other drugs I'm taking?
- Will I be able to drive while taking it?
- Will it make me drowsy or sleepy?
- What are the most common side effects and how long do they last?
- What should I do if I experience side effects?
- What's the right time to take it?
- How long will it take to work?
- How long am I likely to have to take it?

Tricyclic (TCAs) and related antidepressants

Name "Tricyclic" refers to the three linked six-sided rings comprising the molecular structure of these drugs. One of these rings is seven sided in some drugs.

How they work TCAs work by blocking reuptake of the neurotransmitters serotonin and noradrenaline. (See 'How do antidepressants work?' page 70). Some TCAs have a strong sedative effect which can help anxious or agitated patients; those with a lesser sedative effect tend to be better for withdrawn and apathetic patients.

History The first TCA, imipramine, was launched in the late 1950s, quickly followed by amitriptyline. Accounting for just under two thirds of all UK anti-depressant prescriptions in the 1980s and early 1990s,[4] these two "old faithfuls" are still widely prescribed.

Effectiveness TCAs are among the most effective of all antidepressants. It may take 10 to 14 days for them to start working and up to six to eight weeks to work fully.[5] Unaware of this, many patients stop treatment before it starts to "kick in" especially if they experience side effects without any benefit. This is not the only problem. Under dosing accounts for some treatment failures. Between 10 and 20 per cent of patients don't respond to TCAs and related antidepressants.[6]

Side effects The most common ones are mentioned below and although they don't affect everyone, they are sometimes severe, especially in the first week or two. They tend to ease with time, so persevering with treatment is worthwhile. Of course, if you are alarmed by the feelings then a chat with your doctor should confirm whether your doseage is correct for you, and whether the effects are unusual or expected.

Common side effects include:

- Blurred vision
- Constipation
- Difficulty passing water
- Drowsiness
- Feeling faint
- Increased appetite
- Loss of libido
- Rapid heartbeat.

Initial low doses may reduce side effects, but increase the time the drug takes to work. TCAs can interfere with diabetes control and heart action and exacerbate epilepsy. Combining TCAs with other drugs can also create problems. Check potential interactions with your doctor.

Overdose Seek immediate medical advice: overdose is extremely dangerous.

Driving TCAs can impair ability to drive or use machinery.

Stopping them Don't do so abruptly. TCAs are not addictive, but can cause unpleasant withdrawal effects such as insomnia, nausea, panic and vomiting. Reducing the dose gradually over several weeks can prevent or reduce bad effects. Seek advice from your doctor.

Comment Newer drugs, such as SSRIs are less toxic and don't cause so many side effects, but *newer* is not always *better. The British National Formulary* says that although newer drugs are better tolerated than older ones the difference is too small to justify always choosing one of the newer drugs as the first line of treatment. This is particularly relevant in cases of severe or chronic depression.

Generic or chemical name Amitriptyline
Brand name(s) Not applicable
Uses Depression, especially if sedation is needed, for example, if depression is accompanied by anxiety or insomnia. Child bedwetting.
Comment The second TCA on the market and for many years the most widely prescribed. Its sedative properties can reduce the need for additional sleeping pills but reduce some patients to a "zombie" like state. Amitriptyline is one of the more dangerous TCAs in overdose and can cause life-threatening heart rhythms and coma.

Generic or chemical name Clomipramine
Brand name(s) Anafranil, Anafranil SR
Uses Depressive illness, especially if sedation is required, panic disorders, phobias, irrational fears, obsessive compulsive disorder, narcolepsy (an uncontrollable sleep-inducing condition).
Comment Powerful, but not a first choice antidepressant; widely used to treat otherwise "refractory "depression (which does not respond to other treatments). First drug to be approved – in 1990 – by the US Food and Drugs Administration for treating obsessive compulsive disorder.

Generic or chemical name Dosulepin/ Dothiepin
Brand name(s) Prothiaden
Uses Depression, especially with anxiety and insomnia.
Comment May relieve anxiety within a few days, but can take several weeks to achieve a full antidepressant effect. It has a lighter sedative effect than amitriptyline, but it may still knock you out cold.

Generic or chemical name Doxepin
Brand name(s) Sinequan
Uses Depression, especially if sedation is needed. Bedwetting in children.
Comment An "old faithful" – often prescribed with sleep in mind.

Generic or chemical name Imipramine
Brand name(s) Tofranil
Uses Depression. Bedwetting in children.
Comment The first TCA, imipramine, is still widely regarded as reliable and effective: less of a sedating effect than other TCAs.

Generic or chemical name Lofepramine
Brand name(s) Gamanil
Uses Depression.
Comment One of the newer TCAs, lofepramine is said to have milder side effects than older agents, to be relatively safe in overdose, and to be particularly well tolerated by elderly patients. Fewer sedative properties than other TCAs. Sweating and constipation are problematic.

Generic or chemical name Nortriptyline
Brand name(s) Allegron
Uses Depression. Bedwetting in children.
Comment Mild sedative properties and can take a long time to work – during which time side effects may increase depression.
Compound or combination products Motival: this combines nortriptyline and fluphenazine.
Uses Depression and anxiety.
Comment Judged to be "less suitable for prescribing."

Generic or chemical name Trimipramine
Brand name(s) Surmontil
Uses Depression, particularly if sedation is needed to treat anxiety, agitation or disturbed sleep.
Comment Another "old faithful". It has a strong sedative effect and usually resolves sleep problems within 24 hours. A true antidepressant effect may occur within seven to ten days.

Tetracyclic antidepressants

"Tetra" (four) refers to the four linked rings characterizing the tetracyclic antidepressants, an extension of the TCA range. The hope that they would produce fewer side effects and increase efficacy have not been fully realized, but they extend prescribing options.

Generic or chemical name Amoxapine
Brand name(s) Asendis
Uses Depression.
Comment Amoxapine has similar effects and side effects to TCAs, but is closely related to the so called major tranquillizers. Side effects may exacerbate depression until it kicks in but it is fast acting, and may achieve an antidepressant effect within four to seven days.

Generic or chemical name Maprotiline
Brand name(s) Ludiomil
Specific uses Depression, especially if sedation is required.
Comment Because it reduces the so called "convulsive threshold" more than other TCAs, it is more likely to induce fits.[7]

Related antidepressants

Generic or chemical name Mianserin
Brand name(s) Not applicable
Uses Depression, especially if sedation is required.
Comment Monthly blood tests recommended for the first three months to check for blood or liver disorders. Blood tests also recommended in the event of fever, sore throat or mouth infection – possible symptoms of a dangerous drug reaction. These factors have meant that Mianserin has not been used as much as it might have been. On the plus side, it has weaker "anticholinergic effects" than many older antidepressants. Thus it is less likely to cause symptoms such as dry mouth, blurred vision, constipation and urinary problems. Also less dangerous in overdose.

Generic or chemical name Trazodone
Brand name(s) Molipaxin
Uses Depression (especially if sedation is required) and anxiety.
Comment. One of the more sedative of the newer drugs, it has hardly any cholinergic effects. Thus, it is less likely to cause symptoms such as dry mouth, blurred vision, constipation and urinary problems. Also reported to be safer for people with heart problems. Priapism (a permanent erection) is a rare complication, in which case it should be discontinued immediately. Its use as a sedative for

sleep disorders has been questioned. Alyson J. Bond and Malcolm Lader say: it is "unpredictable and unreliable and should be used only to treat the primary illness of depression."[8]

Monoamine oxidase inhibitors (MAOIs)

Name Monoamine oxidase inhibitors (MAOIs) act on the same neurotransmitters as TCAs, but in a different way, by blocking their breakdown.

History The first MAOI, iproniazid, originally developed in 1950s as a tuberculosis (TB) treatment, was found, by accident, to lighten mood.

Effectiveness Recommended for combined anxiety/ depression and phobia.

Side effects MAOIs are not used much now because monoamine oxidase is a natural substance which inactivates harmful substances in food. Inhibiting the action of monoamine oxidase in the gut breaches the body's defences – so taking an MAOI means avoiding foods that monoamine oxidase acts against. The long list includes cheese, yeast products (including beer), broad bean pods, pickled food and alcoholic drinks. Ask your doctor for a full list. Also avoid taking any other drugs – including cold cures, cough sweets painkillers and other forms of self-medication – without checking with your doctor. MAOIs can also cause the same kind of side effects as TCAs.

Interactions between MAOI drugs and forbidden foods, drinks and medicines result in side effects such as severe throbbing headache, high temperature and a rapid rise in blood pressure. Another drawback with most MAOIs (except for moclobemide) is that you have to wait two weeks after coming off it before starting another antidepressant (three weeks if switching to clomipramine or impimpramine). MAOIs are for when other options fail.

Generic or chemical name Isocarboxazid
Brand name(s) Not applicable
Uses Depressive illness, panic disorder.

Generic or chemical name Phenelzine
Brand name(s) Nardil
Uses Depression. Mixed anxiety and depression.
Comment: A response may emerge within a week, but a satisfactory response may take four weeks. If no response appears within two weeks, the dose can be increased to a max. 15mg four times a day.

Generic or chemical name Tranylcypromine
Brand name(s) Parnate
Uses Depressive illness, especially with phobic symptoms.

Reversible MAOIs

Generic or chemical name Moclobemide
Brand name(s) Manerix
Uses Depression and social phobia.
Comment Well tolerated and a lot less toxic in overdose and if food restrictions are broken than other MAOIs.

Selective serotonin reuptake inhibitors (SSRIs)

Name Selective serotonin reuptake inhibitors (SSRIs) act by blocking reuptake of one neurotransmitter – serotonin.

History The launch of the first SSRI, Prozac, in 1988, attracted unprecedented media interest. Prozac quickly became a buzz word and the most widely prescribed psychotherapeutic medicine ever.

Effectiveness Because they are a lot safer and easier to take than their predecessors, SSRIs mark a major advance, but they are no more effective than TCAs.

Side effects Compared with TCAs, SSRIs cause less drowsiness, are less likely to cause dry mouth and blurred vision and do not cause weight gain. Most commonly reported side effects are restlessness, insomnia, diarrhea, nausea and vomiting. Dr. Tim Cantopher reports that at least 50 per cent of his SSRI patients experience SSRI related sexual dysfunction to a greater or lesser degree. He writes: "It may last for as long as you take the tablets (plus a short period while the drug gets out of your system). It's not you, it's the tablets and some other antidepressants can do the same thing."[9]

Generic or chemical name Citalopram
Brand name(s) Cipramil
Uses Depression and panic disorder.

Generic or chemical name Escitalopram
Brand name(s) Cipralex
Uses Depression and panic disorder.
Comment Newer drug which may have fewer side effects and be more potent, though this has not conclusively been proven.

Generic or chemical name Fluoxetine
Brand name(s) Prozac
Uses Depression, Bulimia nervosa, obsessive compulsive disorder (OCD).
Comment Fluoxetine has a long half life, one to three days after acute (short term) therapy and four

to six days after chronic (long term) therapy. "Half life" is the time it takes for a drug in the blood to decrease to half of its original dose. What this means in the case of fluoxetine is that traces of it will linger in your body for much longer than other SSRIs – up to six weeks. This could be bad news if you develop side effects. Fluoexetine may also decrease appetite and have a slight stimulant effect.

Generic or chemical name Fluvoxamine
Brand name(s) Faverin
Uses Depression and obsessive compulsive disorder (OCD).
Comment First SSRI launched in worldwide market in 1983; first approved by US Food and Drugs Administration for OCD treatment.

Generic or chemical name Paroxetine
Brand name(s) Seroxat
Uses Depression, obsessive compulsive disorder (OCD), panic disorder, social phobia, post traumatic disorder, anxiety.
Comment Focus of controversy in which it was reported to be addictive – a claim the manufacturers vehemently deny. (See 'Aren't antidepressants addictive?' page 79). First SSRI approved by US Foods and Drugs Administration for treatment of panic disorder and social phobia

Generic or chemical name Sertraline
Brand name(s) Lustral
Specific uses Depressive illness, including accompanying symptoms of anxiety; obsessive compulsive disorder, post traumatic stress disorder in women.
Comment Usually has a slight stimulant effect.

New generation antidepressants

Why are there are so many antidepressant drugs and why are researchers seeking new ones? Because the existing ones often take weeks to work, often don't work at all and cause a wide range of side effects – often unpleasant and disabling. The perfect antidepressant would work as quickly as a painkiller, wouldn't have side effects and would act in a harmonious way on the brain chemicals which regulate mood. Researchers are edging towards this Holy Grail. A new generation of antidepressants has been developed because some people don't respond to antidepressants working on the serotonin system alone. Usually, tweaking serotonin has a knock-on effect that brings the noradrenaline system into line – *usually* but not always. Don't the old fashioned tricyclics tweak both systems? Indeed, they do, but the new drugs have less severe side effects and are less dangerous in overdose.

Generic or chemical name Flupentixol
Brand name(s) Fluanxol
Specific uses Depression (with or without anxiety).
Comment Low dose formulation of a major tranquilizer originally developed to treat psychotic diseases: its effectiveness against depression was discovered quite by accident. Patients often respond to treatment within two or three days. It should be stopped after one week if the response is inadequate.

Generic or chemical name Mirtazapine
Brand name(s) Zispin
Uses Depressive illness.
Comment First licensed for UK use in 1997, it acts on both the noradrenaline and serotonin systems, but it is more selective than other agents, stimulating only one type of serotonin receptor. Strong sedative effect. Reported to be rarely associated with sexual problems, but sometimes produce marked weight gain. Stop taking it, in consultation with your doctor, if two to four weeks does not produce an adequate response.

Generic or chemical name Reboxetine
Brand name(s) Edronax
Uses Depression.
Comment Acts only on the noradrenaline system. Slight stimulant effect. Insomnia can be a problem.

Generic or chemical name Venlafaxine
Brand name(s) Efexor; Efexor XL
Specific uses Depression and generalized anxiety disorder.
Comment First dual action serotonin and norepinephrine (noradrenaline) reuptake inhibitor (SNRJ). Regular blood pressure monitoring is essential when taking this drug.

Mood stabilizers

Used to treat recurrent depression, mania and manic or bipolar depression, mood stabilizers are regarded as a last resort in treatment of recurrent depression. Lithium, the first mood stabilizer to be discovered, has the highest success rate. A naturally occurring salt, it doesn't cure mood swings, but seems to stop them occurring. It'salso one of the most toxic substances used in medicine – there's a fine line between therapeutic effectiveness and toxicity.

Failure to take it is the commonest reason for relapse. Failure to take enough is another significant factor. Many patients are discouraged by side effects which include nausea, abdominal cramps, thirst, a metallic taste in the mouth and mild hand tremor. In addition, increased thirst – a feature of lithium therapy – can encourage consumption of high calorie drinks, leading to weight gain.

Lithium can take up to a year to work fully. Many patients won't wait that long, especially if they experience side effects before feeling any benefits. Many others suffer no side effects at all – or only mild ones. Some people take Lithium for 20 years or more without any ill effect. Because it's a preventative treatment, it's hard to know when to stop it, if at all. Many users relapse if they stop. If this happens and the symptoms return, and you re-start lithium, you may have to wait a year or more to feel the benefits again.

It's all a matter of weighing up the "risk-benefit ratio". In other words, do the potential benefits outweigh the potential risks and the inconvenience of regular monitoring? One report puts the success rate for bipolar depression sufferers at 70 per cent. Alternative mood stabilizers require less frequent monitoring, but have lower success rates. These include carbamazepine (brand name Tegretol) and valproic acid (brand name Depakote).

Additional antidepressants

Generic or chemical name Trytophan
Brand name(s) Optimax
Uses Severe depression of more than two years continuous duration. Prescribing restricted to hospital specialists when other antidepressants have failed, and then only as adjunct to other antidepressants.
Comment Launched in the 1970s, trytophan was withdrawn in 1990 because of links with a severe blood disorder. This was traced to a contaminant which was eliminated. But the manufacturer still recommends blood tests for patients. Prescribers must complete regular safety questionnaires.

Herbal medicines

St John's Wort (SJW) has been used since medieval times to treat mild depression. It has gained popularity in recent years. Dr Norman Rosenthal, one of the world's foremost authorities on Seasonal affective disorder (SAD) has even written a book describing SJW as "Your Natural Prozac".[10] He notes: "In Germany, SJW is the number one antidepressant prescribed by doctors, far outselling Prozac (by more than ten times over)." But SJW is highly controversial. The UK Seasonal Affective Disorder Association (SADA) has expressed concern about the widespread advertising for SJW products, which are widely sold in Britain as over the counter (OTC) products.

SADA says: "Regulation of OTC medicines is very lax. Prescription medicines have to pass many years of stringent trials before being launched but OTC remedies do not. Many SAD sufferers have tried SJW in recent years and SADA has heard many different reactions; some, very positive but others ranging from negative to disastrous, with side effects causing lasting health problems.

SADA was made aware (but not by the companies marketing SJW products) that SJW interacts with bright light and can cause negative symptoms of photosensitivity (sensitivity to light). As the principal clinically-proven treatment for SAD is bright light, this news was potentially alarming."

As no clinical trials of SJW in SAD have been undertaken in the UK, SADA carried out a survey among its members to assess the perceived value of SJW as a treatment for SAD. 2000 questionnaires were sent to SADA members: 308 were returned and 291 were accepted for analysis – a very poor return rate of 15 per cent. The results, however limited they are in what they imply, are as follows:

- **Two thirds of respondents (200) had tried SJW, of whom 70 per cent combined it with bright light treatment and 16 per cent with anti-depressant medication, over an average period of use of 18 weeks.**
- **Just over 40% of users thought it effective or mostly effective.**
- **Just over 30 per cent reported adverse effects, most commonly headaches (13 per cent), sore eyes (11 per cent) and nausea (11 per cent). As feared, some eye reactions caused the most serious adverse effects, lasting weeks, months or even years after discontinuation of SJW, rendering users unable to use bright light treatment or face daylight.**
- **59 per cent said they would use SJW again; 34 per cent said they would not.**

In summary, there is some evidence that St John's Wort can be an effective treatment for mild to moderate depression, however an analysis of studies published in 2004 has concluded that

"SJW may be less effective in the treatment of depression than previously assumed."[11]

It is only sub-syndromal SAD (the mild version of SAD) that falls into the category of mild to moderate depression. The symptoms and features of SAD differ from those of other forms of depression and sensitivity to light is one characteristic of severe SAD, which may render use of SJW impossible.

SJW in its existing OTC formulations interacts with many prescription medications including, it appears from the survey, antidepressant medication. The *British National Formulary* also warns of adverse interactions[12] between SJW and other antidepressant medications – in addition to other medications, including antibiotics, heart drugs and the contraceptive pill. Check with your doctor before taking SJW at the same time as other drugs.

Notes to drug directory

1 Quitkin F., McGrath P., Stewart J. *et al.*, *'Chronological milestones to guide drug change. When should clinicians switch antidepressants?', Archives of General Psychiatry* 1996: 53:785–92.

2 *Drug and Therapeutic Bulletin* 1999; 37: 7.

3 Quitkin F., McGrath P., Stewart J. *et al.*, 'Chronological milestones to guide drug change. When should clinicians switch antidepressants?', *Archives of General Psychiatry* 1996; 53:785–92.

4 Lacey R., *The Complete Guide to Psychiatric Drugs: A Layman's Handbook.*

5 *The British Medical Association New Guide to Medicines and Drugs,* Dorling Kindsersley, 1997.

6 *British National Formulary*, No. 46. September 2003.

7 Bond A. and Lader M. *Understanding Drug Treatment in Mental Health Care*, John Wiley and Sons, 1996.

8 Ibid .

9 Cantopher T, *Depressive Illness: The curse of the strong,* Sheldon Press, 2003.

10 Rosenthal N., *St. John's Wort, Your Natural Prozac,* Thorsons, 1998.

11 Werneke U., Horn O., Taylor D., *How effective is St. John's Wort? – The evidence revisited,* 2004.

12 British National Formulary, No. 46. September 2003

Further information

Part One

Useful contacts

Depression Alliance,
35 Westminster Bridge Road,
London, SE1 7JB.
information@depressionalliance.org
www.depressionalliance.org
Provides information and advice; runs local self-help groups and maintains directory of allied organizations.

Manic Depression Fellowship,
Castle Works, 21 St. George's Road, London SE1 6ES.
Tel: 020 7793 2600.
mdf@mdf.org.uk
www.mdf.org.uk
Provides information, including legal and employment advice; runs self-help groups and self-management training programmes.

MIND (The National Association for Mental Health), 15–19 Broadway, London E15 4BQ.
Tel: 020 8519 2122.
contact@mind.org.uk
www.mind.org.uk
Promotes needs of people with mental health problems; provides information and advice about mental health issues; and runs more than 200 local MIND associations in England and Wales.

National Childbirth Trust,
Alexandra House, Oldham Terrace,
London W3 6NH.
Tel: 0870 444 8707.
enquiries@national childbirth trust.co.uk
Provides information about sources of help for post natal depression.

Royal College of Psychiatrists,
17 Belgrave Square,
London SW1X 8PG.
Tel: 020 7235 2351.
rcpsych@rcpsych.ac.uk
www.rcpsych.ac.uk
Provides mental health information for healthcare professionals and the general public.

SADA – Seasonal Affective Disorder Association , PO Box 989, Steyning,
West Sussex.
www.sada.org.uk
Provides information; runs local groups and hires light boxes.

Further reading

A User's Guide for Patients and Families. The Antidepressant Sourcebook, Andrew L. Morrison, Main Street Books, Doubleday, 2000.
The author is an American psychiatrist.

British National Formulary. British Medical Association and the Royal Pharmaceutical Society of Great Britain. September 2003.
A prescribing guide for doctors which lists available drugs, their licensed uses, recommended doses and side effects. Regularly updated. Also available on the internet.
www.bnf.org *

The South London and Maudsley NHS Trust 2003 Prescribing Guidelines. David Taylor, Carol Paton, Robert Kerwin. Martin Dunitz, 2003.*
One of a series of reference books designed to promote informed prescribing in psychiatry.

Winter Blues. Seasonal Affective Disorder: What It Is and How To Overcome It, Norman E. Rosenthal. Guildford, 1993.
Written by an American sufferer who is also a doctor and leading researcher.

Feelings after Birth. The NCT Book of Postnatal Depression, Heather Welford, NCT Publishing, 2002.
Comprehensive guide published by the National Childbirth Trust.

Breakdown: a personal crisis and a medical dilemma, Stuart Sutherland. Oxford University Press, 1998.
A leading British psychologist describes his own experience of manic depressive illness and writes about psychotherapy, drugs and their effects on the brain; and the nature and origins of mental

illness.

Mental Illness: A handbook for carers, R. Ramsay, C. Gerada, S. Mars and G. Szmukler. Jessica Kingsley Publishers, 2001.
Written in recognition that friends and relatives of people who suffer from depression also need help and advico.

Malignant Sadness: The Anatomy of Depression, Lewis Wolpert. Faber, 1999.
A personal account of depression with a scientific perspective by a leading British biologist. *(See case history, page 83)*

Darkness Visible: A Memoir of Madness, William Styron. Vintage Books, 1990.
A book which began as a lecture. Styron describes his experience of a crippling kind of illness.

Part two

Useful contacts

British Association for Behavioural and Cognitive Psychotherapists
Globe Centre
PO Box 9, Accrington, BB5 2GD
Tel: 01254 875277.
Fax: 01254 239114.
babcp@babcp.com
www.babcp.org.uk
Maintains a register of members who have to present detailed information about training and experience, supported by another qualified practitioner. Bound by ethical standards, including supervision and continuing professional education.

UK Council for Psychotherapy
167–169 Great Portland Street, London WIN 5PF.
Tel: 020 7436 3002.
ukcp@psychotherapy.org
www.psychotherapy.org.uk
Umbrella body with about 90 member organizations representing all main psycho-therapeutic traditions. The Royal College of Psychiatrists and the British Psychological Society are represented on the Council. More than 4,500 (accredited) psychotherapists were registered with the Council in 2003. All accredited therapists train to postgraduate level and agree to conform to the Council's ethical guidelines. The Council sets agreed training criteria for all of its member organizations. There is free access to the register database to find psychotherapists:

- In your local area
- Who practice a particular type of psychotherapy
- Who have wheelchair access
- Who are based outside the UK.
- Who belong to a particular member organization.

British Association for Counselling and Psychotherapy
1 Regent Place, Rugby, Warwickshire CV21 2PJ.
Information line: 0870 443 5252 (Mondays to Fridays 8.45am-5pm)
mailto:bac@bac.co.uk
www.counselling.co.uk
Maintains nationwide directory of accredited private counsellors, plus information on choosing a counsellor. Telephone or send SAE to above address or use online directory.

Further reading

Cognitive Therapy and the Emotional Disorders, Aaron T. Beck. Penguin, 1976.
The original guide (for both psycho-therapists and the general public) by the godfather of cognitive therapy.

The Feeling Good Handbook, Dr David Burns. Plume, 1999. More than 700 pages from a US psychiatrist – everything from depression and anxiety, fears and fears, phobias to interpersonal communication and self esteem.

Mind over Mood, Dennis Greenberger and Christine Padesky. Guilford Press, 1995. Self-help guide by two US clinical psychologists, with emphasis on case histories, work sheets and practical exercises.

Cognitive Therapy for Depression and Anxiety, Ivy-Marie Blackburn and Kate Davidson, Blackwell Science Ltd., 1995.* Textbook for practitioners by two of the leading British names in the field.*

What Works for Whom? A Critical Review of Psychotherapy Research, Anthony Roth and Peter Fonagy. Guildford, 1996. Academic evaluation of research by a clinical psychologist and a psychoanalyst.*

Technology in Counselling and Psychotherapy, Stephen Goss and Kate Anthony (eds). Palgrave Macmillan, 2003.* Innovative and broad-ranging guide for therapists by a wide range of British and US contributors.

Counselling and Psychotherapy: A Consumer's Guide, Windy Dryden and Colin Feltham. Sheldon Press, 1995. A British response to the ever increasing demand for "talking therapies".

** Written for a professional or academic readership rather than the general reader.*

Computer-aided packages

*Beating the Blues (*for anxiety and depression). Beating the Blues (computerised cognitive behavioural therapy for anxiety and depression). Developed jointly by Ultrasis plc and Dr.Judy Proudfoot from the Institute Institute of Psychiatry, King's College, London. Available at some GP surgeries. For more information, go to http://www.ultrasis.com or Tel: 020 7600 6777.

Restoring the Balance (Mental Health Foundation, 2000) Based on cognitive behaviour therapy techniques, this CD includes interactive exercises and is designed for people with mild to moderate anxiety or depression. For more information, go to www.mentalhealth.org.uk or call 020 7802 0302 during office hours.

Good Days Ahead: Initially designed for use under clinical supervision: a self-help version for home use is now available. Professional actors portray characters overcoming anxiety and depression. For more information go to www.mindstreet.com or Tel: 001 502 893 9271.

Bibliography

Association of the British Pharmaceutical Industry, *Target Depression,*1999

4th American Psychiatric Association, *Diagnostic and Statistical Manual of Mental Disorders,*1994.

Trevor Barnes, *Dealing with Depression,* Vermillion, 1996.

Aaron T. Beck, *Cognitive Therapy and the Emotional Disorders,* Penguin Books, 1989.

Glin Bennett, *Patients and their Doctors,* Secker and Warburg, 1979.

Ivy Marie Blackburn and Kate Davidson, *Cognitive Therapy for Depression and Anxiety,* Blackwell Science, 1995.

Alyson J. Bond and Malcolm H. Lader, *Understanding Drug Treatment in Mental Health,* John Wiley & Sons Inc.,1996.

British Medical Association and the Royal Pharmaceutical Society of Great Britain, *British National Formulary,* September 2003.

David Burns, *The Feeling Good Handbook,* Plume,1999.

Tim Cantopher, *Depressive Illness, The curse of the strong,* Sheldon Press, 2003.

Rita Carter, *Mapping the Mind,* Phoenix, 1998.

Anthony Clare, *Psychiatry in Dissent: Controversial Issues in Thought and Practice,* Tavistock Publications, 1976.

Gerald C. Davison, *Abnormal Psychology,* and John M. Neale, John Wiley & Sons Inc., 1998.

Windy Dryden and Colin Feltham, *Counselling and Psychotherapy,* A Consumer's Guide, Sheldon Press, 1995.

Max Fink, *Psychobiology of Convulsive Therapy,* Winston and Sons, 1974.

Paul Gilbert, *Overcoming Depression: a self-help guide using Cognitive Behavioural Techniques,* Robinson Publishing Ltd., 1997.

Stephen Goss and Kate Anthony (eds), *Technology in Counselling and Psychotherapy. A Practitioner's Guide,* 2003.

Dennis Greenburger and Christine Padesky, *Mind over Mood,* Guilford Press,1995.

Sarah Harvey and Ian Wylie, *Patient Power,* Simon and Schuster, 1999.

Ron Lacey, *The Complete Guide to Psychiatric Drugs: A Layman's Handbook,* Ebury Press, 1991.

Fresher Pressure: How to survive as a student, Aidan Macfarlane and Ann McPherson, Oxford Paperbacks, 1994.

Vicky Maud, *Stress and Depression in children and teenagers,* Sheldon Press, 2002.

Spike Milligan and Anthony Clare, *Depression and How to Survive It,* Ebury Press, 1993

Andrew L. Morrison, *The Antidepressant Sourcebook: A User's Guide for Patients and Families,* Main Street Books, Doubleday, 2000.

Brice Pitt, *Down with Gloom, Or How to Defeat Depression,* Gaskell,1993.

R. Ramsay, C. Gerada, S. Mars and George Szmukler, *Mental Illness: A handbook for carers,* Jessica Kingsley Publishers, 2001.

Richard S. Stern and Lynne M. Drummond, *Treatment of Depression. Practice of Behavioural and Cognitive Psychotherapy,* Cambridge University Press, 1991.

Norman E. Rosenthal, *Winter Blues. Seasonal Affective Disorder: What It Is and How To Overcome It,* Guilford Press, 1998.

Anthony Roth, *What works for whom? A Critical Review of Psychotherapy Research,* and Peter Fonag, Guilford, 1996.

Hans Selye, *Stress Without Distress,* Lippincott and Crowell, 1974.

Stephen Stahl, Essential Psychopharmacology of Depression and Bipolar Disorder, Cambridge University Press, 2000

William Styron, *Darkness Visible: A Memoir of Madness,* Vintage Books, 1990.

Stuart Sutherland, *Breakdown: A personal crisis and a medical dilemma,* Oxford University Press,1998.

David Taylor, Carol Paton, Robert Kerwin, *The South London and Maudsley NHS Trust 2003 Prescribing Guidelines,* Martin Dunitz, 2003.

Alan Watkins (Editor), *Mind Body Medicine: A Clinician's Guide to Psychoneuroimmunology,* Churchill Livingstone, 1997.

Heather Welford, *Feelings after Birth, The NCT book of Postnatal Depression,* NCT Publishing, 2002.

J. Mark, G. Williams, *Treatment of Depression: A Guide to the Theory and Practice of Cognitive Behaviour Therapy,* Routledge, 1992.

Malignant Sadness: The Anatomy of Depression, Lewis Wolpert, Faber,1999.

Telepsychiatry and e-Mental Health, Richard Wootton, Peter Yellowlees and Paul McClaren.

The British Medical Association New Guide to Medicines and Drugs, Dorling Kindsersley, 1997.

Index

Permissions

Page 20: Ghaemi S.N., Miller C.J., Berv D.A., Klugman B.A., Pies R., 'Sensitivity and specificity of a new bipolar spectrum diagnostic scale.' *Journal of Affective Disorders* 2004; in press. Reproduced with permission of Dr Ronald Pies.

Page 26: Extract from *Depression and How to Survive it* by Spike Milligan and Anthony Clare, published by Ebury. Used by permission of The Random House Group Ltd.

Page 36/37: Holmes T. and Rahe R., 'The Social Readjustment Rating Scale', from *The Journal of Psychosomatic Research*, 11(2): 213–218 © 1967 Elsevier Inc. Reprinted with permission from Elsevier.

Page 58: Case history 'The sadness that dares not speak its name'. Reprinted with permission from e-mental-health.com

Page 65: 'The Patient's Code' was first published in *The Expert Patient* by John Illman. Reprinted with permission of the ABPI.

Page 67: Case history 'The psychiatrist's story'. Anon: *Psychiatric Bulletin*, 1990; 14: 452–454. Extract reproduced with the permission of The Royal College of Psychiatrists.

Page 90: Case history: 'ECT', pp. 217–218. *Breakdown: a personal crisis and a medical dilemma* 2nd edition by Stuart Sutherland (1998). Reproduced by permission of Oxford University Press

Page 105: 'Factors in childhood history leading to depressive schema' p.33. *The psychological treatment of depression. A guide to the theory and practice of Cognitive Behaviour Therapy*, J., Mark G. Williams, Routledge, 1992. Reproduced by permission of Routledge.

Page 117: (Pre and post-therapy activity schedules). *Treatment of Depression: The Practice of Behavioural and Cognitive Psychotherapy*, R.S. Stern, L.M Drummond, Isaac Marks, Cambridge University Press. 1991. Reproduced by permission of Cambridge University Press.

Page 118: 'Behaviour diary'. p.121. J. Mark, G. Williams, *The psychological treatment of depression. A guide to the theory and practice of Cognitive Behaviour Therapy*, Routledge, 1992. Reproduced by permission of Routledge.

Page 118, 131 and 132: Images used by permission of *Beating the Blues,* Ultrasis plc.

Page 71: 'Sinks' concept and pictures reproduced courtesy of Dr Tim Cantopher, author of *Depressive Illness: the curse of the strong,* Sheldon Press, 2003.

Acknowledgements

I am extremely grateful to the following who gave me their wisdom, expertise and time.

Firstly, my son James, a psychologist, for his unflagging help with research, Rita Carter, for her unobtrusive editing and little gems, and for inviting me to write the book in the first place, Anna Cheifetz and Joanne Wilson for their patience and professionalism at Cassell, Dr Kate Cavanagh, Dr Rachel Mycroft, Dr George Szmukler, Louise Collins and Dr David Taylor for reading the text and for their many constructive comments. Thank-you to Satwan Singh for his insightful interview and Jo Trosh, for the case history featuring *Beating The Blues*. Thanks also to Dr Norman Rosenthal, a writer I have greatly admired for many years, for his personal case history and the many other people with depression who shared their experiences with me. Finally thanks to Isaacs Marks who introduced me to the concept of computerized cognitive behaviour therapy at a lecture in 2003.

Many thanks also to Liz, Chris and other members of the family for their support – especially Dad who died in February 2004, from Parkinson's disease, as the manuscript was nearing completion, for his selflessness.

Publishers acknowledgements

The author and publisher gratefully acknowledge the permission granted to reproduce the copyright material in the book. Every effort has been made to trace copyright holders and to obtain permission for the use of copyright material. The publisher apologizes for any errors or omissions and would be grateful if notified of any corrections that should be incorporated in future reprints or editions of this book.

Picture credits